THIS IS
A BOOK FOR
PEOPLE
WHO LOVE

The Royals

Running Press
Hachette Book Group
1290 Avenue of the Americas, New York, NY 10104
www.runningpress.com
@Running_Press

Printed in China

First Edition: October 2020

Published by Running Press, an imprint of Perseus Books, LLC, a subsidiary of Hachette Book Group, Inc. The Running Press name and logo is a trademark of the Hachette Book Group.

The Hachette Speakers Bureau provides a wide range of authors for speaking events. To find out more, go to www.hachettespeakersbureau. com or call (866) 376-6591.

The publisher is not responsible for websites (or their content) that are not owned by the publisher.

Text by Rebecca Stoeker.

Print book cover and interior design by Jenna McBride.

Library of Congress Control Number: 2020935701

ISBNs: 978-0-7624-7084-6 (hardcover), 978-0-7624-7086-0 (ebook)

RRD-S

10 9 8 7 6 5 4 3 2 1

THIS IS
A BOOK FOR
PEOPLE
WHO LOVE

REBECCA STOEKER

ILLUSTRATIONS BY MONIQUE AIMEE

RUNNING PRESS
PHILADELPHIA

Dedicated to...

My mom, who is my favorite partner in
unremitting royal enthusiasm.

My dad, who has always seen more in me
than I have seen in myself.

And Ms. Wessling, a teacher who believed
I could write and told me, "You can."

Contents

Introduction

The English monarchy is really quite exceptional. It traces its roots back more than one thousand years and is one of the oldest surviving monarchies in the world. Queen Elizabeth II, the current sovereign, is the longest-serving ruler in British history, not to mention one of the longest-serving monarchs in all of world history. Her reign began on February 6, 1952, after the sudden death of her father King George VI. She has ruled for over sixty-eight years, surpassing the former record of sixty-three years held by Queen Victoria. Exceptional, indeed!

All of this, however, leads to a question that is often asked: What has allowed the British monarchy to survive this long, especially when so many other European monarchies collapsed during the twentieth century? What allowed the British royals to continue flourishing—and the British people to maintain their affection for the ruling family? The answer lies in the ability of British royals to balance beloved traditions with an eye toward adaptability. British royalty is steeped in tradition, some of which dates back hundreds upon hundreds of years. There's a degree of predictability that provides a feeling of stability in an ever-changing world. And the world *has* changed—drastically. But through all of those changes—some exciting, some mundane—the crown (the monarch and the monarchy itself) must be seen as something set apart. If it becomes too modern and relatable, it loses its power, but if it remains too aloof, it loses its credibility. The monarchy's ability to adapt to shifting social norms and technology, while at the same time maintaining a firm hold on tradition, has kept it not only alive, but thriving.

While many members of the current royal family have played a role in keeping its image strong and relevant, no one has been a more pivotal figure in this endeavor than Queen Elizabeth II. Her devotion to duty and serving her people has been nothing short of astounding. On her twenty-first birthday in 1947, the then Princess Elizabeth made an incredible promise to her people, declaring that, "my whole life, whether it be long or short, shall be devoted to your service and the service of our great imperial family to which we all belong."

Within five short years of this declaration, she would be queen.

The Queen has clung to tradition and royal protocol throughout her life, but has been forced to bend along the way—sometimes voluntarily and other times involuntarily. Keeping the monarchy fresh and modern, while also keeping it royal and set apart from quotidian life, has  been a balancing act during her entire reign. Her husband Prince Philip and others have advised her to make changes over the decades—some she accepted, others she did not. After all, she alone is the Queen, and in the end, she has the final say. If the past sixty-eight years have proven anything, it's that Queen Elizabeth knows a thing or two about when to stand up and when to back down.

Much of her enormous popularity—and the survival of the British monarchy in general—lies not just in balancing tradition and adaptability, but in remaining staunchly, unfailingly neutral about politics. The Queen and the monarchy as a whole are meant to be above politics. As

Prime Minister Winston Churchill said in 1953, "It is natural for Parliaments to talk and for the Crown to shine." The monarchy stands as a unifying force for the people, a symbol of continuity and security rather than a beacon of political ideology. And for the monarchy to thrive—and, crucially, for it to continue to be seen by the people as a necessary institution worthy of their attention—it must win the hearts of as many of its subjects as possible.

Politics, especially today, can create large chasms of disagreement that lead to anger and frustration—the monarchy's job is to unify, not divide. When royal family members begin pushing political agendas, it can (and has in the past) caused many to question their legitimacy. People, unsurprisingly, do not want to support an institution monetarily that goes against their own political beliefs.

The Queen has been an incredible example of what it means to stay above and out of politics. Certainly in private she has her own political beliefs. But her public tact and neutrality have helped endear her to the British public in a way that other members of the royal family can only dream of. They have also made her more relatable—unique as that may seem, when we're speaking about a queen—to a much wider array of people. Thanks to the Queen's example, keeping political beliefs private is one of the foundations that the monarchy depends on for its survival.

Today, Britain's monarchy continues to thrive in an age of constant transformation and changing expectations. Queen Elizabeth II continues as a prevailing symbol of stability, security, and permanence, in the United Kingdom and around the world. But how did the monarchy get where it is today? Who are the characters who built this institution? What are today's royals doing? And what sort of fabulous perks do they have behind those palace walls? Read on to peek behind the monarchy's tastefully appointed velvet curtains!

Royal History

Queen Victoria & Prince Albert

The British royal family traces its roots back almost a millennium. This is too small of a book to cover that entire familial history, much as we would love to! But many would argue that Queen Victoria's reign is the proper place to begin the story of the modern royal family. Queen

THIS IS A BOOK FOR PEOPLE WHO LOVE THE ROYALS

Victoria is similar to the current sovereign, in that neither of them was ever supposed to rule. Victoria was the daughter of Prince Edward, Duke of Kent, the fourth son of King George III, and her father died before she was even a year old. Victoria's grandfather died before her first birthday as well, and his third son William IV (Victoria's uncle) ascended the throne. Neither William IV nor his elder brothers produced any surviving, legitimate heirs, so at barely eighteen years of age, after the death of her uncle, Victoria became queen of the United Kingdom.

Luckily, Queen Victoria was fortunate enough to marry for love. She had met her cousin Prince Albert in 1836 at the age of seventeen when he traveled from Germany to visit England. Her uncle, King Leopold I of the Belgians—who also happened to be Prince Albert's uncle—was very much in favor of the pairing and encouraged it—you can think of him as a bit of a royal matchmaker. Victoria wrote to Leopold on June 7, 1836, to thank him for arranging the meeting, saying, "Allow me, then, my dearest Uncle, to tell you how delighted I am with him, and how much I like him in every way. He possesses every quality, that could be desired to render me perfectly happy... He has besides, the most pleasing and delightful exterior and appearance, you can possibly see."

It was not until October 15, 1839, however, that the pair became engaged—with Queen Victoria asking Prince Albert to marry *her*, since she held the higher royal status. Prince Albert was equally smitten with the queen, penning a romantic note in November following their engagement that gushed, "Your image fills my whole soul. Even in my dreams I never imagined that I should find so much love on earth." The pair married on February 10, 1837, in the Chapel Royal at St. James' Palace.

The royal couple would go on to have nine children: Princess Victoria (Vicky), Prince Albert (Bertie), Princess Alice, Prince Alfred, Princess Helena, Princess Louise, Prince Arthur, Prince Leopold, and Princess Beatrice. Several married into the various royal families of Europe, with Queen Victoria eventually gaining the charming unofficial title "Grandmother of Europe." By 1914, her grandchildren were either monarchs or married to monarchs in eight European countries.

Today, monarchs all over Europe trace their ancestry directly back to Queen Victoria and Prince Albert, including both Queen Elizabeth II and Prince Philip of Great Britain, King Felipe VI of Spain, King Harald V of Norway, Queen Margrethe II of Denmark, and King Carl XVI Gustaf of Sweden.

Sadly, the royal love story would end tragically, with Prince Albert dying in 1861 at the relatively young age of forty-two. Victoria would go on living another forty years, but would never recover from his death, grieving him for the rest of her life.

King Edward VII & Queen Alexandra

Prince Albert Edward, known as "Bertie" to the family, was the eldest son of Queen Victoria and Prince Albert. He married Princess Alexandra of Denmark in 1863. The royal couple would go on to have six children, with five living to adulthood: Prince Albert Victor, Prince George, Princess Louise, Princess Victoria, and Princess Maud. The marriage was not a very happy one, with Bertie having numerous extramarital affairs, the most enduring of which was with Alice Keppel (interestingly, Keppel would have a great-granddaughter with even more royal connections: Camilla Parker Bowles, now the Duchess of Cornwall). Bertie became King Edward VII upon his mother's death

 in 1901. His reign was relatively short. After decades as the Prince of Wales, waiting in the wings to finally ascend the throne, he passed away on May 6, 1910, after ruling only nine years.

King George V & Queen Mary

The heir to the throne should have been Prince Albert Victor, known as Prince Eddy, but the young prince had died at the age of twenty-eight, on January 14, 1892, after contracting influenza and pneumonia. Prince Eddy had become engaged to his cousin, Princess May of Teck, about a month before on December 3, 1891 (both were great-grandchildren of King George III). Queen Victoria had been very much in favor of the match and delighted with the prospect of Princess May as a granddaughter-in-law. When Prince Eddy asked Princess May to marry him, it was the first time the pair had ever been alone together. While Princess May was shocked and distressed by the prince's death, it is difficult to gauge how much she could have truly loved him, since the two had spent so little time together.

The burden of being third in line to the throne—and thus the successor to the ultimately short-reigned King Edward VII—suddenly shifted from Prince Eddy to Prince George. With his elder brother's death, his marriage suddenly took on tantamount importance. It was vital that he wed and produce an heir to continue the royal line. The public was very fond of Princess May, and both the British people and the royal family were in favor of her becoming engaged to Prince George. It was understandably a rather awkward situation for the two at first. But over the course of many months, as they shared their grief over Eddy's death and exchanged many friendly letters, the relationship blossomed into a romance. Prince George asked Princess May to marry him sixteen months after Eddy's death. The couple joined in matrimony on July 6, 1893—another successful love match for Victoria's line.

The two went on to have six children: Prince Edward (known as "David" in the family), Prince Albert (known as "Bertie"), Princess Mary, Prince Henry, Prince George, and Prince John. The elder Prince George ascended the throne upon his father's death in 1910, and the couple became King George V and Queen Mary. The pair helped guide the nation through the sorrows and hardships of World War I and were also responsible for a stylistic evolution for the monarchy—changing the name of the royal family from the German-sounding House of Saxe-Coburg and Gotha to the more English, patriotic-sounding House of Windsor.

King Edward VIII

Prince Edward, the eldest son of King George V and Queen Mary, became King Edward VIII upon his father's death in 1936, but would reign for less than a year—never even having a coronation. Why, you might wonder? Edward had never wanted to be king; in fact, the very idea terrified him. In 1931, he had met an American divorcee, Wallis Warfield Simpson, who was married to her second husband, Ernest Simpson, at the time. The pair would eventually go on to have a passionate affair, and by 1936, Edward was determined to marry Wallis. However, as king he would also become the head of the Church of England and would therefore never be allowed to marry a divorced woman.

A few months after Edward became king, his controversial relationship with Wallis became public. While he had been popular as the Prince of Wales and subsequently as King Edward VIII, the public did not support the match with Mrs. Simpson—to put it lightly. Public and political pressure mounted for him to either give up his relationship with her or abdicate. But Edward was besotted with Wallis and insisted on marrying her. He made history on

December 11, 1936, when he announced his abdication, declaring in a radio address to the public, "I have found it impossible to carry the heavy burden of responsibility and to discharge my duties as king as I would wish to do without the help and support of the woman I love." The couple went on to marry in France six months later, becoming known as the Duke and Duchess of Windsor.

King George VI & Queen Elizabeth

No one would be more affected by King Edward VIII's abdication than his younger brother Prince Albert (Bertie) and his young family. Bertie was married with two young daughters when Edward abdicated. He had grown up as a shy, quiet boy with a persistent stammer. The idea of being king was in many ways as frightening and repugnant to him as it was to his elder brother, but growing up, the chances of Bertie ever becoming king had seemed exceedingly slim.

In 1916, Bertie met his future wife, Lady Elizabeth Bowes-Lyon, though neither would recall that instance. They met again at a ball at the Ritz Hotel in June 1918, and many more times over the next few years. The prince was drawn to Elizabeth's close, informal, and fun-loving family—which, as you might imagine, stood in stark contrast to the usual tradition and rigidity of the royal family. The pair began writing to each other late in 1920. By early 1921, it was clear that Bertie was besotted with Elizabeth. His parents very much enjoyed Elizabeth's company and were both in favor of the match. Elizabeth, on the other hand, needed a bit more convincing! It would take three proposals to persuade her to accept the prince's hand. The pair finally became engaged in January 1923 and were married at Westminster Abbey on April 26 of that year.

The couple became known as the Duke and Duchess of York. Their eldest daughter, Princess Elizabeth Alexandra Mary, was born on April 21, 1926. She was adored by her parents and both sets of grandparents, but none of them would have dreamed she would one day become the monarchy's longest-reigning queen! Her sister, Princess Margaret Rose, was born on August 21, 1930. The family of four enjoyed a pleasant domestic life at 145 Piccadilly in London. They

were very close and truly loved spending time together. However, this idyllic life was brought to an abrupt end with Edward's abdication in December 1936.

Prince Albert, though terrified of being king and extremely distressed by his brother's decision, understood the importance of duty. He became King George VI immediately following his elder brother's stepping down. Not only had his life changed drastically, but his wife who had originally questioned whether she could handle the pressure of marrying into the royal family at all now found herself as queen consort. Their daughter Princess Elizabeth was only ten years old when she suddenly became heiress presumptive to the throne. The young family that had lived a relatively private and cozy life together was thrust into the spotlight and forced to move to Buckingham Palace.

The new king did not have a lot of time to adapt to his new role before an even bigger crisis hit the country. The rise of Adolf Hitler and Nazism in Germany began to threaten Europe in the mid to late 1930s, and as time passed, it became clear that Hitler would need to be stopped by force. Germany invaded Poland in early September of 1939, and on September 3, Britain declared war on Germany, just twenty-one years after the end of World War I.

The king and queen were now faced with the daunting prospect of leading a nation at war. Throughout the war, the royal couple worked hard to boost morale whenever and wherever they could. Their two young daughters were moved to Windsor Castle for their safety, as London endured constant air raids. Even Buckingham Palace did not escape the devastation and was bombed on September 13, 1940, while the king and queen were in residence. While a horrifying experience, the queen admitted that it allowed her to relate more easily to countless other Londoners who had seen their homes and businesses destroyed by the Luftwaffe.

The war in Europe finally ended with Germany's surrender on May 7, 1945. It had been years longer than most had predicted and was the deadliest war in human history. The bravery, resolve, and kindness of the royal pair throughout the war years had won the hearts of the British people. While the king and queen were anxious to return to a more "normal" life, the war had taken a heavy toll on the king's health, and their happiness would be cut painfully short.

On February 6, 1952, King George VI passed away unexpectedly in his sleep at Sandringham House in Norfolk. His daughter, Princess Elizabeth and her husband, Prince Philip, were on a royal tour in Kenya when she received the news. Shocked and devastated, she was immediately flown back to Britain and became Queen Elizabeth II—at only twenty-five.

Queen Elizabeth II & Prince Philip

Princess Elizabeth Alexandra Mary was the first granddaughter of King George V and Queen Mary. She was doted on as a child and in some ways seemed destined for the crown no one predicted she would ever wear. She was a serious and dutiful child, unlike her younger sister Princess Margaret, who was fun-loving and spoiled.

Princess Elizabeth first met Prince Philip of Greece and Denmark on a visit to Dartmouth Naval College in July 1939, when she was thirteen and he was a handsome eighteen-year-old naval cadet. Princess Elizabeth was immediately smitten with the dashing Philip, and the pair began to exchange letters. Their correspondence continued throughout the war years. Her parents were concerned about her young age and the fact that she had not dated anyone else. They also wondered how the public would feel about Philip's lineage, including the fact that he was not a British subject. But Elizabeth was determined to marry the man she loved, and in August 1946, she accepted Philip's proposal.

After they became engaged, Prince Philip wrote to Elizabeth's mother, Queen Elizabeth, and said, "I am sure I do not deserve all the good things which have happened to me. . . . To have fallen in love completely and unreservedly makes all one's personal and even the world's troubles seem small and petty." It truly was a love match on both sides.

Elizabeth's parents insisted, however, that the couple wait to formally announce their engagement until Elizabeth had turned twenty-one. In the meantime, she accompanied her parents and sister on a tour of South Africa. During their separation, Prince Philip became a naturalized British citizen and was no longer styled as Prince Philip of Greece and Denmark but instead Lieutenant Philip Mountbatten. He also joined the Church of England. The young couple continued their correspondence throughout the tour, falling more in love in spite of the separation—for these young royals, absence truly did make the heart grow fonder.

Their engagement was officially revealed on July 9, 1947. The announcement from Buckingham Palace read: "It is with the greatest pleasure that the King and Queen announce the betrothal of their dearly beloved daughter the Princess Elizabeth to Lieutenant Philip Mountbatten RN son of the late Prince Andrew of Greece and Princess Andrew [Princess Alice of Battenberg] to which union the King has gladly given his consent." The pair was married on November 20, 1947, at Westminster Abbey.

Princess Elizabeth gave birth to the couple's first child, Prince Charles Philip Arthur George, at Buckingham Palace on November 14, 1948, about one week before their first wedding anniversary. Their daughter, Princess Anne Elizabeth Alice Louise, was born on August 15, 1950. Surely the young couple assumed they would have more time before Princess Elizabeth would ascend the throne. But Princess Elizabeth became Queen Elizabeth II upon her father's death in February 1952, with the pair having been married less than five years.

Prince Philip initially struggled in his new role as queen's consort. Their royal duties massively increased once she became the monarch, diverting their attentions and shifting the dynamic of their relationship. However, both eventually became accustomed to their new roles, and they went on to have two more children: Prince Andrew Albert Christian Edward (born February 19, 1960) and Prince Edward Antony Richard Louis (born March 10, 1964).

Queen Elizabeth II and Prince Philip have been married for over seventy years. They have eight grandchildren and eight great-grandchildren. The couple has faced some incredible personal challenges, including the very public divorces of three out of four of their children, a fire that destroyed much of Windsor Castle, and the tragic death of Diana, Princess of Wales. While their marriage has faced its share of hardships, they have found a way to weather each storm and find strength in each other. The Queen's former private secretary, Lord Charteris, once said, "Prince Philip is the only man in the world who treats the Queen simply as another human being. He's the only man who can. Strange as it may seem, I believe she values that." The Queen stated in 1997, after fifty years of marriage, that Prince Philip "has, quite simply, been my strength and stay all these years, and I, and his whole family, and this and many other countries, owe him a debt greater than he would ever claim, or we shall ever know."

Queen Elizabeth II has reigned longer than any other British monarch in history. She has met twelve US presidents and seen her country through some extraordinarily challenging times. She has remained a bulwark of strength and stability for her nation and the Commonwealth for almost seventy years.

The Line of Succession

AND

Royal Family Tree

The Royal Line of Succession

As the last chapter shows, succession is a critically important aspect of the monarchy—and one that can lead to some
exciting and unexpected turns in the course of history!
Traditionally, succession in the royal family has followed
the rule of male-preferred primogeniture. In other—less
fancy—words, the crown is always passed through the male
line, unless there are only female children. For example, had
King George VI and Queen Elizabeth had a son—regardless of birth order—he would have become king and there
never would have been a Queen Elizabeth II. But because
the couple only had daughters, Princess Elizabeth and
Princess Margaret, the crown passed to the eldest daughter.
Had the Queen Mother given birth to a son, it would not
have mattered if he were younger than his sisters. Simply
by virtue of being male, he would have become the heir—
and any subsequent brothers would have pushed Elizabeth
and Margaret even further down the line of succession.

This is why there have been so few queens in British
history. Male heirs were always preferred, and royals worked
hard to make sure they produced one. However, as Winston

Churchill said in a radio broadcast upon the death of King George VI and the accession of Queen Elizabeth II, "Famous have  been the reigns of our queens. Some of the greatest periods in our history have unfolded under their sceptre."

In the twenty-first century, male-preferred primogeniture seems antiquated at best and discriminatory at worst. The Queen is a remarkable monarch, who has known when to hold fast to tradition but also when to modernize—and that includes her response to the line of succession. In 2012, she announced the end of male-preferred primogeniture in the royal line of succession—made official by the 2013 Succession to the Crown Act. Her timing was, as usual, impeccable. Why? It ensured that if Prince William and Catherine ("Kate") Middleton, who had been married the year before, had a baby girl as their firstborn child, that baby would retain her place in the line of succession, regardless of any royal brothers later on. We now know that the Duke and Duchess of Cambridge's first child was Prince

George. He follows his father directly in the line of succession. However, the Cambridges' second child was Princess Charlotte, born in 2015. While she will most likely never rule Great Britain, as a result of the change in 2013 she keeps her place in the royal line of succession despite the birth of her younger brother Prince Louis in 2018.

While the 2013 Succession to the Crown Act has altered the rules for children born after its establishment, it did not change the line of succession for those born *before* it was passed. For example, Princess Anne was the second child of Queen Elizabeth II and Prince Philip, but her two younger brothers Prince Andrew and Prince Edward are before her in the line—as are their children. The more children born to direct heirs of the throne, the

further down the line other royal family members are pushed. For example, Prince Andrew was pushed down the line of succession by the two sons of Prince Charles—Prince William and Prince Harry. Those who marry into the royal family, such as Kate Middleton, will never be a part of the line of succession. The current line as of the end of 2019 follows the order given here. But as a younger royal generation continues to have children, the line will continue to change and adjust—just like the monarchy itself.

1	His Royal Highness the Prince of Wales (Prince Charles)
2	His Royal Highness the Duke of Cambridge (Prince William)
3	His Royal Highness Prince George of Cambridge
4	Her Royal Highness Princess Charlotte of Cambridge
5	His Royal Highness Prince Louis of Cambridge
6	His Royal Highness the Duke of Sussex (Prince Harry)*
7	Archie Harrison Mountbatten-Windsor
8	His Royal Highness the Duke of York (Prince Andrew)
9	Her Royal Highness Princess Beatrice of York
10	Her Royal Highness Princess Eugenie of York

11	His Royal Highness the Earl of Wessex (Prince Edward)
12	James, Viscount Severn
13	Lady Louise Windsor
14	Her Royal Highness the Princess Royal (Princess Anne)
15	Peter Phillips
16	Savannah Phillips
17	Isla Phillips
18	Zara Tindall
19	Mia Tindall
20	Lena Tindall

*While the Duke and Duchess of Sussex have chosen to "step back" from royal duties, that does not affect Prince Harry's, or his son's, place in the line of succession. He has chosen, however, to longer use his HRH styling.

Royal Titles

AND

Greetings

Deciphering Royal Titles!

Titles within the royal family and British nobility can appear—and are—quite complicated! The system for ranking members of the British aristocracy is known as the peerage. According to Debrett's London, one of the leading authorities on the history of the peerage system, "A peer of the realm is someone who holds one (or more) of five possible titles . . . inherited from a direct ancestor or bestowed upon him by the monarch." A "peer of the realm" was originally someone who swore allegiance to the monarch in exchange for money or property. The peerage has historically been made up of very powerful nobles, who remained strong and firmly connected through blood and marriage. Their security was directly connected to the

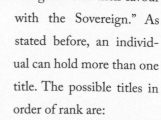

"stability of the kingdom and their favour with the Sovereign." As stated before, an individual can hold more than one title. The possible titles in order of rank are:

Duke

Marquess

Earl

Viscount

Baron

While some titles are bestowed, others are inherited, but almost always through the male line. Being royal is not a requirement for being a member of the peerage, though royal peers are of course the most well-known. The Queen's husband and three sons all hold peerage titles. Unfortunately, keeping afloat amidst the confusion of royal titles and their history can be harder than navigating the English Channel! My advice? Keep calm and carry on!

It is tradition for male members of the royal family to be granted a new title upon their marriage. For example, Prince William, who had been known simply as Prince William of Wales, was given the title Duke of Cambridge by his grandmother the Queen after his marriage to Catherine

Middleton in 2011. Catherine, therefore, became the Duchess of Cambridge.

However, men who marry *into* the royal family do not usually receive a title. For example, Jack Brooksbank did not receive a title when he married Princess Eugenie, the Queen's granddaughter, in 2018. There are exceptions of course, such as when the Queen's sister Princess Margaret married Antony Armstrong-Jones in 1960. The Queen granted him the title Earl of Snowdon and Princess Margaret became the Countess of Snowdon.

There are titles that are part of the royal family only and do not technically belong to the peerage. The monarch, obviously, is known as either king or queen and outranks any other title. The spouse of the king or queen is known as the "consort." For example, the wife of a king is known as the queen consort.

The titles of prince and princess belong only to children of the monarch and grandchildren of the monarch through the male line, as well as to the firstborn son of the eldest son of the Prince of Wales—in this case, Prince George, whose father Prince William is the eldest son of

Charles, Prince of Wales. That was a royal mouthful! Take a moment to chew on that before you swallow! This rule may seem a bit cumbersome to us today, but it dates back to the Letters Patent of 1917 issued by King George V.

However, despite this rule, the monarch can offer the titles of prince or princess to others within the royal family. Confused yet? The best way to address all of the many intricacies of royal titles is through an old-fashioned question and answer session! Below you will find some of the most commonly asked questions regarding royal titles, along with answers that will hopefully make things much clearer!

Why do Princess Charlotte and Prince Louis have titles?

This is a great question and a common one, since it appears to directly contradict the Letters Patent of 1917. On December 31, 2012, the Queen issued a Letters Patent of her own which stated:

> *The Queen has been pleased by Letters Patent under the Great Seal of the Realm . . . to declare that all the children of the eldest son of The Prince of Wales should have and enjoy the style, title and attribute of Royal Highness with the titular dignity of Prince or Princess prefixed to their Christian names or with such other titles of honour.*

In other words, all the children of Prince William, regardless of gender or birth order, would receive the title of His/Her Royal Highness and would be styled as either a prince or princess. Therefore, each of the three children of the Duke and Duchess of Cambridge have the title of HRH and prince or princess. Before this, it would have only been Prince George as the eldest son of the eldest son of the Prince of Wales who would have been entitled to being styled as HRH Prince George of Cambridge. Keep in mind that this only applies to the children of Prince

William, as the eldest son of the Prince of Wales. It does *not* apply to the children of Prince Harry.

Why isn't Catherine Middleton called Princess Catherine?

Catherine would have had to have been born with the title of princess in order for her to use it *before* her name. While she is often referred to as "Princess Kate" in the media, that styling is incorrect. The late Princess of Wales was also commonly referred to as Princess Diana, but that was also incorrect. Her correct title was Diana, Princess of Wales. The only way for Catherine to accurately have the word *princess* before her name is if she were referred to as Princess William of Wales, which, strange as it sounds, is a correct styling. When a woman marries into the royal family, she takes on the title(s) of her husband. So Catherine not only became the Duchess of Cambridge; she also became Princess William of Wales—this may seem a bit clunky, but think of it as similar to when a woman marries and the couple is referred to as Mr. and Mrs. John Smith.

Why aren't Princess Anne's children called prince or princess?

Princess Anne is the *daughter* of the monarch; therefore, her children are not entitled to titles. Titles are only passed down through the *male* children of the monarch. This means that Princess Charlotte's children will not be guaranteed titles either. The Queen worked to change that rather antiquated rule, however, when her daughter's children, Peter and Zara Phillips, were born. She offered the titles of prince and princess to Princess Anne for her children. However, Princess Anne turned down the offer, preferring her children to have no royal titles and thus ensuring they would live a more normal life. Titles can be and are at times refused.

Why do Princess Beatrice and Princess Eugenie have titles?

Both Princess Beatrice and Princess Eugenie are grand-children of the monarch through their father Prince Andrew, the Queen's third child and second son. As grandchildren of the monarch through one of the male lines, they are allowed the title of princess. However, when they marry, their spouses do not take on the title of prince. The titles of female members of the royal family to not automatically transfer to their husbands the way the titles of male members of the royal family transfer to their wives. For example, Prince Harry was made the Duke of Sussex upon his marriage to Meghan Markle and she automatically became the Duchess of Sussex. When Princess Eugenie married Jack Brooksbank, however, he did not take on her title by becoming a prince.

If and when Princess Beatrice or Princess Eugenie has children, those children will not automatically be granted royal titles. Only a prince can pass down his title. Titles might be offered by the reigning monarch to their children, but since Prince Charles is in favor of streamlining and simplifying the monarchy, it is rather unlikely he would grant any once he takes the throne.

If Princess Beatrice and Princess Eugenie have the title of princess, shouldn't Lady Louise Windsor?

Lady Louise Windsor (technically, Mountbatten-Windsor) is the daughter of Prince Edward, the Queen's youngest son. According to the rules of titles (which are often bent), yes, Lady Louise could have been given the title of princess and her brother James, Viscount Severn, could have been given the title of prince. When Prince Edward married Sophie Rhys-Jones in 1999, most expected that he would be made a duke, as is the custom for the male children of the monarch upon their marriage. However, he was instead named Earl of Wessex. In the statement announcing his new title Buckingham Palace made clear that Prince Edward would take the title Duke of Edinburgh upon his father's death and his brother's ascension to the throne.

The statement also said that the Queen had decided, with the approval of Edward and Sophie, that their future children would not be styled as His/Her Royal Highness nor would they be a prince or princess. They would instead be given titles reflective of children of an earl. Therefore they are known as Lady Louise Windsor and James, Viscount Severn, rather than HRH Princess Louise of Wessex and HRH Prince James of Wessex. It is unclear why this particular decision was made. Perhaps Edward and Sophie wanted to follow Princess Anne's lead and give their children a more normal life. Or perhaps the decision came as a result of Prince Charles's push for a more streamlined royal family.

Why is Prince Charles known as the Prince of Wales?

The title of Prince of Wales is bestowed (in other words, it is not inherited and you cannot be born with it) by the reigning monarch on a male heir apparent to the throne. The heir apparent is usually the eldest son of the monarch, but in some cases, the eldest son has passed away and therefore the second son of the monarch or even grandson has been granted the title. Females are only given the title "Princess of Wales" if they marry the Prince of Wales. "Princess of Wales" is a courtesy title rather than a title held outright. For example, when the Queen was Princess

Elizabeth, she never would have been granted the title of Princess of Wales. But when Diana married Charles, she took on his title and became the Princess of Wales.

Why is Princess Anne known as the Princess Royal?

Finally, an easy answer! This is a title bestowed (again, one is not born with this title nor can it be inherited) on the eldest daughter of the monarch. Princess Anne is the eldest and only daughter of the Queen and the Duke of Edinburgh. When the Queen was simply Princess Elizabeth and her father was King George VI, she was never given the title of Princess Royal because her aunt, Princess Mary, already held the title.

Why isn't Prince Philip called a king?

The wife of a reigning monarch is called a queen consort, whereas the husband of a reigning monarch is known as a prince consort. Prince Philip was not crowned at the Queen's coronation. However, Queen Elizabeth (the Queen

Mother) was crowned at the coronation of her husband, King George VI (this will be explained in greater detail in the chapter on royal events, see page 53). Because the title of "king" carries a higher rank than "queen," it would not be appropriate for Prince Philip to be called "King Philip" considering he is not the monarch. While he had been Prince Philip of Greece and Denmark, he was not crowned a prince of the United Kingdom until 1957, four years after the Queen's coronation, when she issued a Letters Patent stating: "The Queen has been pleased . . . to give and grant unto His Royal Highness the Duke of Edinburgh, K.G., K.T., G.B.E., the style and titular dignity of a Prince of the United Kingdom of Great Britain and Northern Ireland, Whitehall."

Why doesn't the Duke and Duchess of Sussex's son, Archie, have a title?

According to the Letters Patent of 1917, Archie is not entitled to a royal designation of prince . . . yet. He could have taken on his father's earldom and been known as Archie,

Earl of Dumbarton, but that was clearly not the wish of his parents, who announced his name simply as Archie Harrison Mountbatten-Windsor. Harry and Meghan, through not giving their son a title, are signaling their wish for him to grow up living a more normal, private life. Archie might become a prince when Prince Charles becomes king. According to the Letters Patent of 1917, children of the monarch and grandchildren of the monarch through the male line are entitled to the styling of prince or princess. This is unlikely, however, considering Prince Charles's wish to continue to restructure and simplify the monarchy and the desire of the Duke and Duchess of Sussex to "step back" from royal duties and keep their son's life more private.

Why does Archie have the last name of Mountbatten-Windsor?

At first glance, Archie's surname seems a bit out of left field. It left many confused when it was first announced! But the last name of Mountbatten-Windsor was established in 1960 and is the surname used by lesser members of the royal family who don't have a royal title. It is seen as a nod to the Duke of Edinburgh's heritage, who, before marrying the Queen, was known as Philip Mountbatten. The current royal family is known as the House of Windsor. And many within the royal family simply use "Windsor" as their surname (for example, Prince Edward's daughter is generally known as Lady Louise Windsor, not Lady Louise Mountbatten-Windsor, though technically that is her full surname). According to the official website of the royal family,

The Queen and The Duke of Edinburgh decided that they would like their own direct descendants to be distinguished from the rest of the Royal Family. . . . It was therefore declared . . . that The Queen's descendants, other than those with the style of Royal Highness and the title of Prince/Princess, or female descendants who marry, would carry the name of Mountbatten-Windsor.

What does "stepping back" from royal duties mean for the Duke and Duchess of Sussex and their titles?

When the Duke and Duchess of Sussex announced in January 2020 that they would be "stepping back" from royal duties, no one was fully clear on what that meant. The Queen, Prince Charles, Prince William, and Prince Harry worked together, along with palace staff, to come up with a plan for the Duke and Duchess to take on a more private, normal life. The Sussexes had expressed their wish to "step back as 'senior' members of the Royal Family, and work to become financially independent." Becoming "financially independent" is a major issue for any member of the royal family, because they cannot be seen to be making a profit off of their royal status (in this case, the Sussex Royal brand). But one of the most important questions asked during the fallout was about Harry and Meghan's royal titles. Would they keep their titles? Would they keep their HRH styling?

After what became known as the "Showdown at Sandringham," between Harry and members of his family, Buckingham Palace made an announcement:

> *As agreed in this new arrangement, they [the Sussexes] understand that they are required to step back from royal duties, including official military appointments. They will no longer receive public funds for royal duties. . . . The Sussexes will not use their HRH titles as they are no longer working members of the Royal Family.*

The couple will now be known as Harry, Duke of Sussex, and Meghan, Duchess of Sussex. However, they have not been "stripped" of their HRH status. They will simply no longer be using that styling. What that means in practical terms has yet to be seen. It is worth noting that Prince Harry, by virtue of being born into the royal family and receiving his HRH status at birth, cannot ever have his HRH title taken away (just as King Edward VIII did not lose his HRH status when he abdicated the throne in 1936). Meghan technically could have hers removed, as both the Duchess of York and Princess of Wales had their

HRH statuses removed after their respective divorces. But it wouldn't make sense to strip Meghan of her HRH status while still married to Harry.

Ex-royal press secretary Dickie Arbiter pointed out that Harry is doing the "honourable" thing by not using his HRH styling anymore. "Harry is not using his HRH because it would be a conflict of interest should he decide to embark on commercial enterprises. Harry knows full well that it is wrong to trade on your name." Royal historian and author Penny Junor stated: "I think holding onto it is very, very good because it means that if something was to happen in the future, and who knows what might happen in the future, circumstances might change and they might want to come back. They might want to do royal work again, they might be needed. I think not to burn bridges is a good thing. It does mean that they won't be able to cash in, one would hope, on their royal status."

There are still many issues to be worked out in this situation and many questions left to be answered. Over the coming months and years, the Duke and Duchess of Sussex will continue to carve out a new role for themselves, and only time will tell what that will look like.

Greeting a member of the Royal Family

Now that you hopefully understand how titles work, suppose you were to have the pleasure to actually meet a member of the royal family? There are not any true requirements when meeting a royal. No one is required by law, for example, to bow to the Queen. However, many do wish to follow traditional practices and codes of conduct.

FOR MEN: The traditional greeting is a bow of the head, though a handshake is also acceptable.

FOR WOMEN: The traditional greeting is a small, quick curtsy—not the grand, low curtsy to the floor common in Disney movies! Women, however, may also prefer to stick to a simple handshake.

Keep in mind, however, that refusing a bow of the head or a curtsy to members of the royal family might be interpreted by others as an anti-monarchical slight.

As for addressing members of the royal family, their official website gives full instructions:

> *On presentation to The Queen, the correct formal address is "Your Majesty" and subsequently "Ma'am," pronounced with a short "a," as in "jam". For male members of the Royal Family the same rules apply, with the title used in the first instance being "Your Royal Highness" and subsequently "Sir". For other female members of the Royal Family the first address is conventionally "Your Royal Highness" and subsequently "Ma'am".*

Greetings within the Royal Family

While the public has choices as far as how to greet members of the royal family, those within the family must follow a stricter set of guidelines in how they greet one another, and it all depends on royal rank. This can all be quite a bit to learn, especially for someone marrying into the royal family, and no one wants to be the one to inadvertently ruffle royal feathers by using the wrong address or bowing to the wrong person! The Queen, of course, holds the highest rank, followed by her husband, the Duke of Edinburgh. And it is relatively easy to determine the rank of those born into the royal family, but with individuals who marry into it, the hierarchy can get rather complicated!

In 2012, the Queen updated the Order of Precedence, which now requires women who marry into the royal family to curtsy to blood princesses when not accompanied by their spouse. Blood princesses are those born into the royal family, including Princess Anne (the Queen's daughter), Princess Alexandra (the Queen's cousin), and Princess Beatrice and Princess Eugenie (the Queen's granddaughters through Prince Andrew). As we've noted previously, women who marry into the royal family reflect the rank of their husbands.

This can all be a little befuddling—think of how the family members must feel!—so let's look at an example: the Duchess of Cambridge would be required to curtsy to Princess Eugenie if not accompanied by Prince William. However, if Kate is with William, she takes on his rank, thus outranking every blood princess. The same applies to the Duchess of Cornwall or the Duchess of Sussex. Though Camilla, Duchess of Cornwall, is married to the heir apparent to the throne, she is still required to curtsy to blood princesses if not accompanied by Prince Charles.

As far as the style of the bows or curtsies, they are the same for royals as for commoners greeting members of the family: a relatively quick curtsy for women or bow of the head for men. These royal greetings apply in public and supposedly in private. But if the Duchess of Sussex comes over by herself for a cousin playdate between Archie and the Cambridge children, would she curtsy to the Duke and Duchess of Cambridge upon arrival? Who knows?

Royal Events

Royal Weddings

Few events give royalty a chance to show off like a royal wedding. And no one does tradition and pomp like Great Britain! British royal weddings are not only a chance for the nation to celebrate, but in many ways the whole world. The British royal family continues to capture the imagination of billions. Royal weddings have always been full of tradition, beauty, romance, and glamour.

Queen Victoria & Prince Albert

It is hard to calculate how many of our traditions and societal mind-sets were influenced by the reign of Queen Victoria. When a monarch rules for sixty-three years over one of the most powerful nations on earth, there will be lasting impacts, and her wedding on February 10, 1840, is no exception. She kept a detailed diary her whole life and wrote of her wedding day like any young, glowing bride, full of excitement, love, and admiration for her handsome prince: "I felt so happy when he placed the ring on my finger. As soon as the Service was over, the Procession returned as it came, with the exception that dearest Albert led me out!"

The royal bride started a new tradition that has carried on to this day: wearing white for her wedding day. Talk about a trendsetter! While not the first royal bride in history to ever wear white, it is Queen Victoria who is credited with making the tradition stick. It was a bold choice for the time period, however, as it was seen as a color of mourning. It would be like a bride wearing black to her wedding today; it has happened, but is extremely rare. It was also seen as too reserved a color and the bride was criticized by some at the time, but Queen Victoria had something more important in mind than pleasing her critics. She had chosen white as the best color to display the lace on her gown, which had all been made by British lace makers who were struggling financially. The young queen wanted to give the lace-making industry in Britain a boost with her patronage.

The royal bride was also criticized for not wearing a crown or robes trimmed in ermine, as would have been befitting of a queen. However, in typical Queen Victoria fashion, she boldly went where no one had gone before and chose a simple wreath of orange blossoms, which matched the embroidered orange blossoms on the train of her gown. She did wear some jewelry, however, including a diamond necklace and earrings as well as a sapphire brooch Prince Albert had given her as a wedding gift.

The couple was married at the Chapel Royal at St. James' Palace and greeted along the processional route from Buckingham Palace by crowds of well-wishers. Queen Victoria wrote that, "I never saw such crowds as there were in the Park, & they cheered most enthusiastically." The bride also wrote in her diary about the ceremony, saying it was, "very impressive & fine, yet simple." The pair had a wedding feast afterward and then traveled to Windsor Castle, where they enjoyed a short but sweet three-day honeymoon. The groom had wanted a two-week honeymoon, but the bride insisted that she could only take a very short break from work. Unfortunately, a set number of vacation days are not always guaranteed when you are queen!

Prince Albert & Lady Elizabeth Bowes-Lyon

The parents of the current queen, Prince Albert (Queen Victoria's great-grandson and later King George VI) and Lady Elizabeth Bowes-Lyon, were married on April 26, 1923, at Westminster Abbey. The day of their wedding they were given the titles of the Duke and Duchess of

York. Lady Elizabeth wore a dress designed by Madame Handley-Seymour, a former dressmaker for Queen Mary, that was surprisingly ill-fitting and, frankly, rather frumpy. It was a dropped waist gown and her veil was attached around her forehead—both in typical 1920s fashion.

Lady Elizabeth unknowingly began a tradition that would be followed by subsequent royal brides when she placed her bridal bouquet on the Tomb of the Unknown Warrior inside the abbey, an act most likely commemorating her brother Fergus Bowes-Lyon, who had been killed during World War I. Every royal bride since has followed the tradition, including Queen Elizabeth II and Kate Middleton. The newly married Duke and Duchess of York set off on their honeymoon to Polesden Lacey, a country house owned by mutual friends in Surrey. They also spent some time at the bride's Scottish home of Glamis Castle. The pair would become King George VI and Queen Elizabeth after the abdication of King Edward VIII in December 1936.

Princess Elizabeth (Queen Elizabeth II) & Prince Philip

Princess Elizabeth and Prince Philip were married at Westminster Abbey on November 20, 1947. The pair had become secretly engaged in September 1946, shielding their sweet romance from the ever invasive press as the young princess embarked on a royal tour of South Africa with her sister and parents. The pair exchanged many letters during this time, counting down the days until they could be together and let the world know of their love for each other. This secret engagement also meant that when the young couple officially announced their intent to marry almost a year later, Princess Elizabeth had turned 21, which her father had added as a stipulation to their marriage. Philip had given his fiancée a diamond and platinum engagement ring which he had designed with diamonds from a tiara that had belonged to his mother. What a sweet gesture! The Queen wears the engagement ring to this day, along with her Welsh gold wedding band.

World War II had been over for two and a half years by the time of the royal wedding. However, the struggle at home was far from over. Rationing continued and large swaths of London remained in ruins from German aerial bombardments during the war. Some felt that a large royal wedding would be out of place in the midst of the nation's continued suffering, but many yearned for a reason to celebrate. The young royal couple filled a war-weary nation with hope for the future, and former prime minister Winston Churchill said that the wedding was, "A flash of color on the hard road we travel." The government eventually agreed to allow a public wedding at Westminster Abbey rather than a private one.

The day of the wedding finally dawned after an engagement that lasted over a year—not unusual for us commoners, but quite lengthy for a royal. A few hours before the wedding, Prince Philip became the Duke of Edinburgh. One of Princess Elizabeth's bridesmaids, the Hon. Pamela Mountbatten, described the couple on their wedding day: "He looked tender, she was adoring." The silk for the bride's wedding gown had been paid for with rationing coupons (many women had sent in their own coupons to try to help pay for the dress, but it would have been illegal for the princess to accept them) and was designed by Norman Hartnell.

Princess Elizabeth carried a bouquet of white orchids along with a sprig of myrtle. The myrtle came from a descendant of a myrtle plant that had been given to Queen Victoria in 1845 by Prince Albert's grandmother and planted at Osborne House, the couple's beloved holiday home on the Isle of Wight. It was Victoria and Albert's daughter, Princess Victoria, who was the first royal bride to use myrtle from this plant in her bridal bouquet. (Myrtle is often associated with love and romance, so it was and is an appropriate choice for a bouquet.) The tradition has continued with royal brides ever since, including Kate Middleton and Meghan Markle. And the sprig in each royal bouquet comes from plants descended from that original gift. How is *that* for royal tradition?

The royal bride chose to wear the Queen Mary's Fringe Tiara for her special day. Unfortunately, even a princess cannot escape the unavoidable mishaps that seem to come with a wedding. While her dresser worked to attach the tiara to her veil, it snapped in half, just hours before the ceremony was to begin! Her mother comforted the princess by assuring her that there were other tiaras to pick from should they be unable to repair it. One thing is for sure,

British royals *never* run out of tiaras. Luckily, jewelry house Garrard was able to make the repair in time for the bride to walk down the aisle on the arm of her proud father.

The ceremony was broadcast by the BBC to around 200 million listeners worldwide. After the ceremony and the carriage procession back to Buckingham Palace, the couple appeared on the balcony to the cheers of thousands. The pair departed later for their honeymoon, which included time spent in Hampshire on the Broadlands Estate owned by Prince Philip's uncle, Lord Mountbatten. They then traveled to Scotland and spent time at Birkhall Lodge on the Balmoral Estate. The royal couple has now been married over seventy-two years.

Princess Margaret & Antony Armstrong-Jones

The Queen's sister Princess Margaret married photographer Antony Armstrong-Jones at Westminster Abbey on May 6, 1960. The pair's romance was not widely known and the engagement took the public largely by surprise when announced in February 1960. Princess Margaret's ruby and diamond engagement ring was designed by her fiancé and supposedly shaped like a rosebud in honor of her middle name Rose.

The bride wore a stunning organza ball gown designed by Norman Hartnell, the same designer who had created her sister's wedding dress thirteen years earlier. The dress itself was relatively simple, but accentuated the princess's tiny waist. It was accessorized with a large veil and the sparklingly enormous Poltimore Tiara. Touchingly, Princess Margaret was escorted down the aisle by her brother-in-law Prince Philip, since her father King George VI had passed away eight years before.

The ceremony was the first royal wedding in Britain to be broadcast on TV and reportedly garnered around 300 million viewers. The royal couple made the traditional appearance on the Buckingham Palace balcony following the ceremony to greet the large, excited crowd of well-wishers. They later departed on a six-week honeymoon around the Caribbean on the Royal Yacht *Britannia*. Now *that* is a honeymoon done in true royal style.

Prince Charles & Lady Diana Spencer

Prince Charles met Lady Diana Spencer in 1977 while dating her elder sister, Sarah. Diana was born on July 1, 1961, the fourth of five children of Earl Spencer and his wife, Frances (their son, John, had died shortly after birth in 1960). Diana was the third daughter and her younger brother Charles was born in 1964. Her parents separated when she was only six years old in 1967, and growing up with divorced parents had always affected her. She was rather shy but had a love of children, and when she and Prince Charles began dating in 1980, she was working as an assistant at the Young England Kindergarten.

The couple's romance began in the summer of 1980, and following a whirlwind courtship in which Diana was hounded incessantly by the media, they announced their engagement on February 24, 1981. Their courtship was so quick that it left little time for the couple to even see one another! Diana reported to have only seen Charles a total of thirteen times between when they started dating and the day of their wedding. The day their engagement was announced, Diana debuted the stunning sapphire and diamond engagement ring which she had chosen herself from a selection of rings presented to her by Garrard, the crown jeweler. (She supposedly picked it because it was the largest—a thought that any girl can relate to!) Diana was only nineteen years old when the couple announced their engagement, thirteen years younger than Prince Charles.

The pair was married on July 29, 1981, at St. Paul's Cathedral in what was aptly called "The Wedding of the Century." When adjusted for inflation, the day was estimated to have cost $110  million! While royal weddings are traditionally held at Westminster Abbey, St. Paul's was chosen because it could hold the 3,500 wedding guests! The bride's now famous dress was the best-kept secret in the world at the time, designed by David and Elizabeth Emanuel. The gorgeous taffeta and lace ball gown was embroidered with 10,000 pearls and had a twenty-five-foot train! Her veil was an astounding forty feet long, and she chose to accessorize the gown with her family's ancestral tiara, the sparkling Spencer Tiara. Her stunning bridal bouquet matched the grandeur of the gown and included, as per royal tradition, a sprig of myrtle.

The bride departed with her father for the wedding from Clarence House in perfect fairytale style in the Glass Coach. The Cinderella-esque coach was built in 1881 and has been used to transport other royal brides on their wedding days, including Lady Elizabeth Bowes-Lyon in 1923 and Princess Anne in 1973. About 600,000 people lined the streets to cheer the royal couple, with an estimated 750 million watching the iconic wedding on television.

During the ceremony, Diana broke with tradition by *not* promising to "obey" her husband. (Catherine Middleton did the same in her vows to Prince William in 2011.) Her bridal nerves also got the better of her, mixing up Prince Charles's name and calling him "Philip Charles Arthur George" during their vows.

After the ceremony, the now Prince and Princess of Wales traveled in an open landau to Buckingham Palace where they, like many royal couples before them,

appeared smiling on the balcony before the cheering thousands. But this appearance would start a new royal tradition, with the couple kissing in front of the delighted, roaring throng. The couple began their honeymoon at the Broadlands Estate where the Queen and Prince Philip had honeymooned. They then enjoyed a two-week Mediterranean cruise on the Royal Yacht *Britannia* before ending their honeymoon at Balmoral in Scotland.

Prince William & Catherine Middleton

Prince William met the uncommonly beautiful Catherine Middleton in 2001 when they lived in the same residence hall: St. Salvator's at St. Andrews University in Scotland. While the two were friends, it wasn't until Kate appeared in a charity fashion show in early 2002 that William really took notice. She sashayed down the runway in a see-through black lace dress and William was in the front row. He reportedly proclaimed to a friend, "Wow, Kate's hot!"

Kate had grown up in a stable family, the eldest of three children born to Michael and Carole Middleton. Michael had been a flight dispatcher and Carole was an air hostess with British Airways. The couple married on June 21, 1980, and Kate was born less than two years later on January 9, 1982. Her younger sister Pippa was born a year and a half later in 1983 and younger brother James followed in 1987. Michael and Carole were proud and loving parents, and the Middleton home was filled with laughter and stability. In 1987, Carole launched her business Party Pieces, selling party supplies, which today has become a multimillion-dollar company.

William and Kate began dating in 2003. The Middletons provided the quiet, steady, and loving home life that William had always craved. His own parents' fighting and very public separation and divorce had filled his childhood with turmoil and unrest. Once he and Kate started dating, William quickly became a frequent visitor at the Middleton home in Berkshire.

Despite a short breakup in 2007, the couple announced their engagement on November 16, 2010. It was a true fairytale romance that delighted the public: the beautiful commoner marrying her dashing prince. Prince William had proposed to Kate a month before in Kenya with his mother's stunning sapphire and diamond engagement ring. Kate said in their engagement interview that the proposal was "very romantic." William spoke touchingly about his mother during the interview, saying, "She's not going to be around to share any of the fun and excitement of it all—this was my way of keeping her sort of close to it all."

The royal couple married on April 29, 2011, at Westminster Abbey. Kate and her family had stayed at the Goring Hotel in London before the wedding, and she departed that morning with her father in a Rolls-Royce Phantom VI. The stunning bride waved to crowds as the car made its way to the abbey. When the Phantom finally came to a stop outside the magnificent church, the bride stepped out to reveal her stunning satin and lace wedding gown designed by Sarah Burton for Alexander McQueen.

The lace had been made by the Royal School of Needlework, and the workers had been required to wash their hands every half hour to keep from sullying the delicate fabric! What no one saw was that there was "something blue" included in the dress: a small blue ribbon sewn onto the inside by Sarah Burton. The magnificent train of the elegant gown was nine feet long—an incredible length, but nothing compared to Lady Diana's. Kate carried a small bouquet of white flowers, which included the traditional sprig of myrtle along with lily of the valley, hyacinth, and adorably, sweet william.

No wedding dress is complete without some sparkle, and no one does jewels better than the royal family. The bride wore the gleaming Cartier Halo Scroll Tiara loaned to her by the Queen—who had received it as an eighteenth birthday present from her parents. Kate also wore a new pair of diamond earrings, given to her as a wedding gift by her parents, that mirrored the acorn and oak leaf design of the new Middleton family crest.

Kate glided down the aisle on the arm of her father, which at three and a half minutes was no short trip! When the bride finally reached Prince William, he told her how "beautiful" she looked and joked to Michael Middleton that the wedding was "supposed to have just been a small family affair." Considering there were

1,900 guests in the abbey that day, it was far more than a "small" event! There were in reality over two billion guests as people around the world tuned in to watch.

After the ceremony, the smiling newlyweds, who were given the titles of the Duke and Duchess of Cambridge, exited the abbey hand in hand to roaring crowds. They traveled back to Buckingham Palace in the 1902 State Landau, which was the same carriage the Queen and Prince Philip had used after their wedding almost sixty-five years earlier as well as Prince Charles and Princess Diana. It had originally been created for the coronation of King Edward VII.

The couple followed tradition by appearing on the Buckingham Palace balcony and then delighted the excited crowds by kissing not once but twice! That evening they attended a wedding reception hosted by Prince Charles where the newly minted Duchess of Cambridge wore another stunning Alexander McQueen gown in ivory satin. The newlyweds were able to get a much needed break and some privacy when they spent ten days honeymooning on a private island in the Seychelles.

Prince Harry & Meghan Markle

Prince Harry and Meghan Markle's romance was the true modern fairytale. The rules and conventions of the twentieth century would have prevented their courtship. King Edward VIII abdicated in 1936 in order to marry a twice divorced American, Wallace Simpson. Prince Harry's great aunt, Princess Margaret, was prevented from marrying her lover Peter Townsend, who was also divorced. However, belief systems and morals have changed over the years, and the relationship between Prince Harry and Meghan—also a divorced American—was allowed to blossom.

Meghan was born on August 4, 1981, and had grown up in California, the daughter of biracial parents. Her parents unfortunately divorced when she was just six years old, and Meghan lived primarily with her mother Doria Ragland. Her father Thomas Markle was an Emmy-winning lighting director, so her exposure to the Hollywood lifestyle began early. She attended Northwestern University and double majored in theater and international relations. She made various television and film appearances before landing her big role as Rachel Zane on the TV drama *Suits* in 2011. The same year she also married her long-term boyfriend, producer Trevor Engelson, but the pair divorced in 2013.

Harry and Meghan were set up on a blind date in July 2016, and Harry recalled of the meeting, "I was beautifully surprised when I . . . walked into that room and saw her. There she was sitting there, I was like, 'OK, well, I'm really gonna have to up my game!' Sit down . . . and make sure I've got good chat." There was an instant connection between the pair, and they quickly had to, in Harry's words, "get the diaries out and find out how we're gonna make this work." Within a few weeks, the couple flew to Botswana together and enjoyed five days of privacy while getting know one another better.

The pair announced their engagement on November 27, 2017, after dating for fifteen months. Harry had proposed to Meghan on a "cozy night" while the pair was roasting a chicken in their two-bedroom home at Nottingham Cottage on the grounds of Kensington Palace.

Harry said that Meghan's response was an "instant yes" and that she didn't even give him time to finish proposing before happily

accepting. Prince Harry had designed the engagement ring consisting of three diamonds, the center stone being from Botswana and, in a touching tribute, the two stones on either side were from Diana's jewelry collection. Meghan described the ring as "perfect" and the inclusion of stones from his mother as "incredibly special."

The couple married and became the Duke and Duchess of Sussex on May 19, 2018, in St. George's Chapel at Windsor Castle. The bride wore a simple but timeless Givenchy gown designed by Clare Waight Keller to walk down the aisle in front of 600 guests. Her sixteen-foot train had been hand-embroidered with floral motifs to represent each of the fifty-three Commonwealth countries. The bride added to her overall look with Queen Mary's Diamond Bandeau Tiara. Her wedding band was fashioned from a piece of Welsh gold, which is a long-standing tradition for royal brides. As the couple exited the chapel hand in hand, they turned to kiss one another and the awaiting crowds cheered with delight.

The couple departed the chapel in an Ascot Landau pulled by four beautiful Windsor Greys. Windsor Greys are specific carriage horses used by the royal family for state occasions, ceremonies, and other important events—including royal weddings. They have to meet certain size requirements and are chosen for their "temperament and stamina." Their name dates back to the reign of Queen Victoria, when the horses were kept at Windsor. They are now housed at the Royal Mews in London.

For their evening reception at Frogmore House on the Windsor Estate, the Duchess of Sussex wore a stunning evening gown by Stella McCartney. She accessorized it with a large aquamarine ring, given to her by Prince Harry, that had once belonged to his mother, Diana. The couple departed 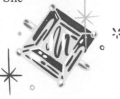 a few days after the ceremony for a honeymoon in an undisclosed location—and no one has ever figured out where they went!

Royal Births

Royal births have always been a cause for great rejoicing and celebration in the UK and beyond. And as is the norm with the royal family, certain traditions are always followed. However, as the years have passed, some practices have gone by the wayside to be replaced by more modern customs.

Traditionally, members of the royal family have always given birth at home. All of the Queen's four children were born at home—though at which royal residence has always varied since there are so many to choose from! However, the Queen's daughter Princess Anne broke with tradition by choosing to give birth to her first child, Peter Phillips, at the Lindo Wing at St. Mary's Hospital in London in 1977. Diana, Princess of Wales, followed suit in 1982, making Prince William the first future monarch to be born in a hospital. Prince Harry was also born at the Lindo Wing, and the Duchess of Cambridge chose to carry on the tradition by giving birth to each of her three children there as well.

Multiple medical professionals are involved with a royal birth, with the Duchess of Cambridge supposedly having around twenty medical staff members to take care of her when Prince George was born. While doctors and nurses are unsurprisingly on hand for a royal birth, it used to be required that another "guest" be present as well, namely the British home secretary! The home secretary would be the official witness to ensure the legitimacy of the newborn royal family member (no switching of royal babies in the delivery room!). Thankfully, this rather awkward tradition was discontinued with the birth of Prince Charles in 1948. Interestingly, royal fathers have not traditionally been present for the births of their children, with Prince Philip playing a game of squash while his wife gave birth to the heir to the throne. While this might seem odd, it is important to keep in mind that societal norms at the time did not require or expect the father to be present. Prince Philip did, however, witness the birth of his fourth child, Prince Edward, in 1964. And royal fathers since, including Prince Charles and Prince William, have attended the births of their children.

For some time, royal women chose to use anesthetics when giving birth. Queen Victoria used chloroform during the birth of her eighth and ninth children, popularizing its use. Queen Elizabeth II also used anesthesia to give birth to three of her four children. The Princess of Wales, however, opted for natural births with her two sons, as did the Duchess of Cambridge with her three children.

Royal births are always highly anticipated by the public, with countless bets being placed on everything from the gender to the name choice! However, the gender is never announced ahead of time (no royal gender reveal parties!) and the name is usually shared days after the birth. The first to be informed of the birth is the monarch. The official announcement to the public is placed on an easel outside Buckingham Palace and usually remains there for twenty-four hours. The crowds outside the palace gates hoping to snap a photo of the historic easel during its brief period on display are immense! However, with the birth of Prince George in 2013, the Duke and Duchess of Cambridge became the first royal parents to share the news through social media. The Duke and Duchess of Sussex followed this trend with the birth of their first child Archie in 2019.

Royal Christenings

As members of the royal family, there isn't really an option of having a christening or not. The Queen holds the title "Defender of the Faith and Supreme Governor of the Church of England" dating back to the reign of King Henry VIII and the Protestant Reformation. Since the sovereign serves as the head of the church, it is essential that any royal baby in the direct line of succession to the throne be christened into it.

As with any other royal event, tradition takes a front-row seat in royal christenings. The current royal christening gown is an exact replica of the one created for Queen Victoria's firstborn Princess Victoria in 1841. The original gown was used by royal babies for over 150 years! Queen Elizabeth, Prince Charles, and Prince William are just a few of the many royal newborns who were dressed in the exquisite Honiton lace gown for their christenings. It was in 2004 that the Queen decided to have a new gown created, since the original had become too fragile. The first to be christened in the new gown was the Queen's grandson, Prince Edward's son James, Viscount Severn in 2007.

Lindo Wing

The Royal Christening Gown

LINDO WING

The Birth Announcement Easel

The Archbishop of Canterbury

Duke and Duchess of Cambridge's Wedding Cake Slice

William & Catherine

Subsequent royal babies, including Prince George, Princess Charlotte, Prince Louis, and Archie Mountbatten-Windsor, have all been christened in the replica gown.

Children of senior members of the royal family are traditionally christened by the Archbishop of Canterbury. This is not a requirement, however, as the Queen was christened by the Archbishop of York. All three Cambridge children were christened by the Archbishop of Canterbury as was baby Archie, the Duke and Duchess of Sussex's son. The ornate Lily Font, like the original christening gown, dates back to the christening of Princess Victoria in 1841. The water used is from the River Jordan where Jesus Christ was baptized. A lovely silver ewer, dating back to the christening of George III in 1738, is used by the archbishop to pour the water over the tiny royal's head.

More recent christenings, including those of the Cambridge children, have been smaller affairs, with just immediate family and godparents in attendance—although royal children usually have quite a few godparents. Prince George has seven, Princess Charlotte has five, and Prince Louis has six. (The Duke and Duchess of Sussex did not allow Archie's godparents' names to be released to the public, so that number is unknown.) The location of royal christenings can vary, with Prince George and Prince Louis being baptized at the Chapel Royal at St. James' Palace in London, while Princess Charlotte was christened at the Church of St. Mary Magdalene on the Sandringham Estate (touchingly, it was the same church where Princess Charlotte's grandmother, Lady Diana Frances Spencer, had been christened many years before).

Following the christening, there is usually a luncheon or tea. Royal couples have traditionally saved the top tier of their wedding cake and served it at the christening of their first child. The Duke and Duchess of Cambridge had enough to serve at the christenings of all three of their children!

Coronations

There exists no other royal event more steeped in tradition and pageantry than a coronation. It is not only a celebration of a new monarch but also an extremely important and serious religious occasion. The ceremony is almost always led by the Archbishop of Canterbury, which dates back to the coronation of William the Conqueror in 1066. The location has been Westminster Abbey for the last 900 years; only two monarchs have not been crowned in the abbey.

The coronation occurs a number of months after the accession of the new monarch to the throne. This allows an appropriate amount of time for mourning the past monarch and for planning the massive event. The ceremony itself is quite lengthy—Queen Elizabeth II's lasted around three hours! The monarch takes a coronation oath, which has changed somewhat over the years. In general, the sovereign promises to reign with mercy and fairness according to the law and to uphold and protect the Church of England.

The monarch sits in King Edward's Chair, which has been used in every coronation since 1626—though the chair itself was made in the year 1300—and is anointed by the Archbishop of Canterbury. The sov-ereign is then crowned with St. Edward's Crown made in 1661 and weighing almost five pounds and partakes in holy communion. As for the spouse of the monarch, the official website of the royal family states,

> *Unless decided otherwise, a Queen consort is crowned with the King, in a similar but simpler ceremony. If the new Sovereign is a Queen, her consort is not crowned or anointed at the coronation ceremony. After the present Queen was crowned The Duke of Edinburgh was the first, after the archbishops and bishops, to pay homage to her.*

Queen Elizabeth II's coronation was held fourteen months after the death of her father on June 2, 1953. It was the first coronation to be televised—an idea championed by the Duke of Edinburgh as head of the Coronation Commission. Twenty-seven million people in the UK  tuned in to watch the historic event. Prince Charles made history as the first child to ever see his mother's coronation, and the ceremony was attended by over 8,000 guests! The Queen wore a breathtaking satin gown with intricate embroidery designed by Norman Hartnell—who also designed her wedding dress. She was driven to the abbey in the Gold State Coach pulled by eight horses, necessary given the enormous weight of the coach. The incredibly ornate coach was completed in 1762 and has been used in every coronation since King George IV. However, the Queen did not enjoy the ride, describing it in a documentary in 2018 as "horrible" and "not very comfortable."

Royal Perks

Royal Tiaras

The British royal family has no shortage of stunning, shimmering headpieces. An entire book could be written on royal tiaras alone. The ten tiaras selected here represent those that have a fascinating history, a strong connection to modern royals, or both. Just imagine which one might look the best atop your own head: it never hurts to dream!

The Cartier Halo Scroll Tiara

This piece is probably one of the most recognizable tiaras in the royal collection today after Catherine Middleton wore it to wed Prince William in April 2011. This stun-

ning tiara was originally purchased by King George VI for his wife Queen Elizabeth in 1936. The Queen Mother did not wear it very often, however, and she later gave it to her daughter as an eighteenth birthday gift. As a princess Elizabeth did not appear to favor the tiara very much, either, choosing to lend it to her sister Princess Margaret, who wore it on several occasions when she was young. When Princess Margaret married, however, she acquired the incredibly large Poltimore Tiara and the Lotus Flower Tiara, which became her more frequent go-to pieces for royal events. The Cartier Halo Scroll Tiara was later worn on a few occasions by Princess Anne when she was young.

The Delhi Durbar Tiara

This ornate tiara was created for Queen Mary to wear to the Delhi Durbar in India in 1911, the ceremony officially recognizing her husband King George V and herself as emperor and empress of India. The original piece contained ten large emeralds along the rim. This tiara is a brilliant example of Queen Mary's over-the-top taste in diamonds and precious stones. As queen, she commissioned countless new pieces of jewelry still in the royal collection. No one could wear as many pieces of jewelry on their person as Queen Mary! She was always finding ways to add on another sparkler to her ensemble. The Delhi Durbar Tiara is one of the largest tiaras in the

royal collection and the first worn by Camilla, Duchess of Cornwall, to a royal event after her marriage to Prince Charles in 2005.

The Girls of Great Britain and Ireland Tiara

This is one of the most iconic tiaras in the royal collection, due to its repeated use by the Queen for depictions on banknotes and stamps. This sparkling headpiece was given as a wedding gift to Queen Mary in 1893. It had been purchased by a committee known as the "Girls of Great Britain and Ireland," who had organized specifically to buy a gift

THIS IS A BOOK FOR PEOPLE WHO LOVE THE ROYALS

for the future queen. Queen Mary wrote a note of sincere thanks to the committee, saying, "I need scarcely assure you that the tiara will ever be one of my most valued wedding gifts as a precious proof of your goodwill and affection." In a touching gesture, Queen Mary gave the tiara as a wedding gift to her granddaughter Princess Elizabeth in 1947, who still refers to it as "Granny's tiara."

Queen Mary's Diamond Bandeau Tiara

The center of this tiara is a stunning diamond brooch that was given to Queen Mary as a wedding gift upon her marriage to King George V in 1893, when they were still the Duke and Duchess of York. In 1932, Queen Mary had the bandeau designed around the brooch, which is still detachable. While the tiara was inherited by Queen Elizabeth II upon her grandmother's death in 1953, it does not appear to have been one of her favorites. The tiara had not been seen in public for decades until Meghan Markle chose to wear the piece for her wedding to Prince Harry in May 2018, giving it new life and popularity.

The Grand Duchess Vladimir Tiara

This piece has a rather lengthy history, originally belonging to Grand Duchess Vladimir of Russia. She fled her country in 1917 at the beginning of the bloody Russian Revolution. The tiara was left behind but eventually smuggled out of the country, with Queen Mary acquiring it upon the death of the grand duchess in 1920. This beautiful tiara, designed with multiple intertwining circles, can be worn with pearl

THIS IS A BOOK FOR PEOPLE WHO LOVE THE ROYALS

pendants, emerald pendants, or no pendants at all. Its versatility makes it unique among the many royal tiaras, and it is a favorite of the Queen to this day. She has worn it countless times since inheriting it up on the death of her grandmother in 1953.

The Lotus Flower Tiara

One of the more recognizable pieces in the royal collection because of its unique Egyptian-inspired design, the Lotus Flower Tiara originally belonged to the Queen Mother. She had it crafted in the 1920s from a necklace her husband had given to her as a wedding gift. Rather than wearing the tiara *on* her head, as is traditional, the Queen Mother wore it around her forehead, a popular look during the Roaring Twenties. She gave it to her younger daughter Princess Margaret in 1959 shortly before her marriage to Antony Armstrong-Jones. It became a favorite of the princess, who loaned it to her daughter-in-law Serena Stanhope for her wedding in 1993. It has more recently been worn by the Duchess of Cambridge on her first appearance at a state banquet at Buckingham Palace, held in honor of China in 2015.

The Oriental Circlet Tiara

This ruby and diamond tiara dates back to the reign of Queen Victoria. It was designed as a gift for her by her beloved Prince Albert, who often designed her jewelry. (A husband who was handsome, thoughtful, and designed

THIS IS A BOOK FOR PEOPLE WHO LOVE THE ROYALS

jewelry? Queen Victoria hit the proverbial jackpot!). The original tiara contained opals rather than rubies. It was a particular favorite of the Queen Mother, who wore it from her early days as queen up until her death in 2002. It was inherited by Queen Elizabeth II and is one of the few ruby tiaras in the royal collection.

Queen Mary's Fringe Tiara

Designed to be worn as either a necklace or a tiara, this royal sparkler first belonged to Queen Victoria and has a strong connection to past royal weddings. Queen Victoria gave it as a wedding gift to her granddaughter-in-law Princess Mary in 1893 when she wed the queen's grandson Prince George. It is probably best known today as the tiara that Queen Elizabeth II wore

on her wedding day in 1947. She and Prince Philip's only daughter, Princess Anne, touchingly chose to wear the tiara for her marriage to Captain Mark Phillips in 1973.

Queen Mary's Lover's Knot Tiara

Often confused and misnamed as the Cambridge Lover's Knot Tiara, this piece was made by Garrard in 1914 for Queen Mary. She wanted the piece to mimic the original Cambridge Lover's Knot Tiara made for her grandmother Augusta, Duchess of Cambridge, in 1818. Queen Mary left the piece to the crown upon her death, with the current monarch inheriting it in 1953. The Queen wore it a number of times early in her reign, but later loaned it to Diana, Princess of Wales, who wore it frequently on royal occasions. The tiara has been given new life over the last few years as a favorite of the Duchess of Cambridge, who has worn it to numerous royal events, including the state visit of US president Donald Trump in 2019. The duchess's frequent use of the tiara is a touching tribute to the mother-in-law she tragically never knew.

The George IV State Diadem

Though technically not a tiara, this crown or diadem is worn frequently by the Queen and is one of the older pieces in the collection. It was originally made for the coronation of King George IV in 1821. It has been worn by

Queen Victoria, Queen Alexandra, Queen Mary, and now Queen Elizabeth II. Consisting of 1,333 diamonds, this sparkler is a true statement piece, and it is unsurprising that the Queen chose to wear it to her coronation in 1953. She also wears it whenever attending the State Opening of Parliament.

THE NIZAM OF HYDERBAD

QUEEN ALEXANDRA'S WEDDING NECKLACE

THE PRINCE ALBERT BROOCH

MAPLE LEAF BROOCH

QUEEN VICTORIA'S CROWN RUBY NECKLACE

THE QUEEN MOTHER'S DIAMOND AND FRINGE EARRINGS

QUEEN MARY'S DIAMOND BAR CHOKER BRACELET

Other Royal Jewels: Baubles, Bangles and Beads!

The jewelry belonging to the British royal family is among some of the most stunning in the world. Many of the pieces have been passed down for generations and have not only a royal, but a sentimental history. The jewelry discussed here has been divided according to type, but the pieces are not listed in any particular order. They have been chosen based not only on their noteworthy past, but also their connection to current members of the royal family.

Necklaces

QUEEN ALEXANDRA'S WEDDING NECKLACE

This lovely pearl and diamond necklace was originally a wedding gift from Queen Victoria's son Prince Albert "Bertie" to his fiancée Princess Alexandra of Denmark (later King Edward VII and Queen Alexandra). The necklace was only one piece in a magnificent set that included a matching tiara, earrings, and brooch. Princess Alexandra wore the necklace on her wedding day in 1863. Many decades later, it became a favorite of the Queen Mother, who wore it numerous times, including for her official eighty-fifth birthday portraits. The current monarch inherited the piece upon her mother's death in 2002, though she has never been seen wearing it publicly. The Duchess of Cambridge gave the beautiful necklace new life in 2018 when she wore it to a state banquet at Buckingham Palace in honor of the Netherlands.

THE NIZAM OF HYDERABAD NECKLACE

One of the grandest necklaces in the royal collection, the Nizam of Hyderabad Necklace was originally designed by Cartier and has a fascinating history. The Nizam of Hyderabad (Asaf Jah VII) gave the then Princess Elizabeth a magnificent wedding gift in 1947: he told her that she could go into Cartier and pick out whatever she wanted—every woman's dream! She chose this beautiful necklace, dripping in diamonds, as well as a glittering tiara—though the tiara was eventually dismantled to create the Burmese Ruby Tiara. The necklace was stunning on the young Elizabeth and just as much of a knockout on the Duchess of Cambridge when she wore it to an event at the National Portrait Gallery in 2014, of which she is patron.

QUEEN VICTORIA'S CROWN RUBY NECKLACE

This scarlet necklace and matching brooch were designed by Prince Albert for Queen Victoria and originally contained opals rather than rubies. The prince often designed jewelry for his beloved wife, with Queen Victoria stating that, "Albert has such taste and arranges everything for me about my jewels." The pieces were created by jewelry house Garrard in 1854. This necklace and brooch were part of the Queen Mother's collection until her death in 2002 and then passed to Queen Elizabeth II. The Queen recently wore the shimmering necklace in 2019 to a state banquet at Buckingham Palace in honor of US president Donald Trump.

PRINCESS DIANA'S ART DECO EMERALD CHOKER

This is one of the most iconic pieces ever worn by the Princess of Wales. Originally given to Queen Mary in 1911, it was shared on a lifetime loan by Queen Elizabeth II with Lady Diana Spencer upon her marriage to Prince

Charles in 1981. Shortly after their wedding, the couple visited Wales where the princess debuted the beautiful emerald choker. In 1984, the Princess of Wales surprisingly but brilliantly chose to wear the choker as a headband around her forehead during a royal visit to Australia, and the photos of her dancing with Prince Charles while wearing the piece are unforgettable.

THE RUBY AND DIAMOND FLORAL BANDEAU NECKLACE

This large V-shaped necklace designed with floral motifs and matching earrings was a wedding gift from Princess Elizabeth's parents in 1947. It is incredibly eye-catching and a true statement piece. The Queen wore the piece early on in her reign, but because of its length, it requires a lower

 neckline to display it properly, and supposedly this is why she has chosen not to wear it in later years. The Queen lent the sentimental piece to the Duchess of Cambridge in 2017, who wore it to a state banquet at Buckingham Palace in honor of King Felipe and Queen Letizia of Spain.

Brooches

THE PRINCE ALBERT BROOCH

The story of this dreamy indigo brooch begins the day before Prince Albert and Queen Victoria married. She wrote in her diary on February 9, 1840, that Prince Albert came up to her room at Buckingham Palace and gave her "a beautiful sapphire and diamond brooch." The blushing bride wore it the next day to her wedding at the Chapel Royal. It was the first of many pieces that the prince would give his beloved wife before his early death in 1861. Victoria adored the brooch and left it to the crown upon her death. Every British queen has worn it since, including Queen Alexandra, Queen Mary, Queen Elizabeth, and Queen Elizabeth II. It consists of a large oval sapphire surrounded by twelve diamonds.

THE FLOWER BASKET BROOCH

This is one of the more intricate and unique of the Queen's brooches and consists of diamonds, emeralds, rubies, and sapphires shaped into, you guessed it, a glittering flower basket design. It has a very sweet history, having been given to then Princess Elizabeth by her parents King George VI and Queen Elizabeth to celebrate the birth of her first child  and their first grandchild Prince Charles in November 1948. The doting new mother wore the brooch for a series of photographs of her and her new son, taken by famed royal and fashion photographer Cecil Beaton. She has worn it countless times since, and it continues to be a distinctive, eye-catching piece.

QUEEN MARY'S TRUE LOVER'S KNOT BROOCH

The Queen owns many bow brooches in her collection, but this one is perhaps the most famous. She inherited it from her grandmother Queen Mary in 1953. Its name alone makes it a sentimental piece to wear to weddings. The Queen wore it to her sister Princess Margaret's wedding to Antony Armstrong-Jones in 1960. She also fittingly chose to wear it to the wedding of her grandson Prince William to Catherine Middleton in 2011, pairing it with a beautiful pale yellow coat.

THE MAPLE LEAF BROOCH

Perhaps the most recognizable of the Queen's brooches, this piece was passed on to her upon her mother's death in 2002. The brooch was originally given to the Queen Mother by her husband King George VI in 1939 for their first royal tour of Canada. She then lent it to her daughter Princess Elizabeth in 1951 for *her* first royal tour of Canada. In 2011, the Queen loaned the sparkling brooch to her new granddaughter-in-law the Duchess of Cambridge to wear on her and Prince William's first tour of Canada as royal newlyweds. The Duke and Duchess of Cambridge paid another visit to Canada in 2016, along with their two young children Prince George and Princess Charlotte, where the duchess was seen once again wearing the lovely brooch. The Queen has also lent the brooch on occasion to the Duchess of Cornwall.

WILLIAMSON CARTIER FLOWER BROOCH

This brooch is truly unique, containing at its center the world's most perfect and largest pink diamond. The diamond was given to Princess Elizabeth as a wedding gift in 1947 by Dr. John T. Williamson, who owned the diamond mine in Tanzania where it was discovered. During her coronation year in 1953, she had Cartier create a brooch

to show off the stunning gem. She has worn it countless times since, including in some adorable photos taken of her and her two children Prince Charles and Princess Anne in 1954. It is a truly sentimental piece, as the Queen has chosen to wear it to a number of important weddings in her life. She wore it to two of her sons' weddings: the wedding of Prince Charles to Lady Diana Spencer in 1981 and the wedding of Prince Edward to Sophie Rhys-Jones in 1999. She also wore the glittering pink brooch to the wedding of her nephew—Princess Margaret's son—Viscount Linley, to Serena Stanhope in 1993.

Bracelets and Earrings

QUEEN MARY'S DIAMOND BAR CHOKER BRACELET

As the name suggests, this piece was originally worn as a choker by Queen Mary. She eventually gave it to her daughter-in-law Queen Elizabeth, the Queen Mother, who had it shortened and made into a bracelet. However, the piece had not been seen since Queen Mary's death in 1953 until the Queen Mother wore the bracelet in her official eightieth birthday portraits in 1980. Upon her death in 2002, the bracelet was passed to Queen Elizabeth II, who has lent it on several occasions to the Duchess of Cambridge. Significantly, the duchess wore it to attend her first state banquet at Buckingham Palace in honor of China in October 2015. It was also worn on the duke and duchess' first royal visit to Paris in 2017.

QUEEN ELIZABETH'S DIAMOND WEDDING BRACELET

This diamond and platinum art deco bracelet has a romantic history, as it was a wedding gift given to Princess Elizabeth by her fiancé Prince Philip, in 1947. Prince Philip used diamonds from a tiara that his mother had given him, which, coincidentally and sentimentally, had been given to *her* as a wedding gift, to create the bracelet. The Queen still wears it often to this day, especially on important occasions such as the State Opening of Parliament and has also worn it for many official portraits, including those taken for her Diamond Jubilee in 2012. She has also touchingly lent it on several occasions to the Duchess of Cambridge, a sign of her trust and affection for the young woman who married her grandson. The duchess paired the bracelet with Queen Mary's Diamond Bar Choker Bracelet for the state banquet in honor China in 2015 and also wore it to the BAFTAs in 2017.

PRINCESS DIANA'S BUTTERFLY EARRINGS

These unique diamond and yellow gold studs originally belonged to the Princess of Wales, who wore them on a royal tour of Canada with Prince Charles in 1986. In a sweet tribute to the mother-in-law she sadly never knew, the Duchess of Sussex chose to wear the earrings on her first appearance after announcing her pregnancy, which was on her first royal tour with Prince Harry to Australia in 2018. The duchess also wore the earrings in 2019 when launching her fashion line, Smart Set, to benefit the charity Smart Works.

THE QUEEN MOTHER'S DIAMOND AND FRINGE EARRINGS

These delicate earrings dripping with diamonds from central sapphires once belonged to the Queen Mother. They are among the most beautiful in the royal collection and have been worn on occasion by the Duchess of Cambridge in a touching tribute to her husband's late great-grandmother. The duchess first appeared wearing them at the 100 Women in Hedge Funds Gala in 2015. She wore them again in 2019 at a state banquet at Buckingham Palace in honor of the president and first lady of the United States.

THE QUEEN'S DIAMOND CHANDELIER EARRINGS

Another set of earrings on loan to the Duchess of Cambridge from the Queen, these sparklers have a stunning chandelier design. She has worn them on numerous occasions since marrying into the royal family, the first time in 2011 when she and Prince William visited Los Angeles. She also wore the earrings for the state visit in honor of China in 2015 and the Royal Variety Performance while pregnant with Prince Louis in 2017.

Buckingham Palace

Windsor Castle

Kensington Palace

The Royal Yacht Britannia

The Palace of Holyroodhouse

Sandringham House

Balmoral Castle

Home Sweet Home: Royal Residences

The royal family has numerous homes. Some are known as "official royal residences" while others are privately owned. The official residences belong to the monarch because of the role of king or queen, while private residences are owned by the royal family and do not receive any public funding. Many of these residences date back hundreds of years.

Buckingham Palace—Official Royal Residence

Perhaps the most famous of all royal residences is Buckingham Palace, the Queen's official home in London. Its iron and gold gates, large balcony, and imposing facade are iconic to London and millions of people travel to the UK every year to see it. The history of the site of Buckingham Palace dates back to the early seventeenth century under the reign of King James I. The house and land were then owned by the Dukes of Buckingham from 1698 to 1762—thus the name we know today. In 1762, the land and house were purchased by King George III as a private home for his family. At the time, the official London residence of the monarch was St. James' Palace.

It was under the reign of King George IV that Buckingham House became a palace and took on its "U" shape. But the work was not completed in his lifetime, and his successor, William IV, had no wish to live there. It was under Queen Victoria that the iconic balcony was added, and she would be the first monarch to truly use Buckingham Palace as an official royal residence.

Buckingham Palace is a colossal residence, though much is hidden from public view. According to the royal family's official website, Buckingham Palace "has 775 rooms. These include 19 State rooms, 52 Royal and guest bedrooms, 188 staff bedrooms, 92 offices, and 78 bathrooms." It's no wonder that the name was changed from Buckingham *House* to Buckingham *Palace*! It is far from just a home, not only in size but in its uses. It is the site of countless receptions, state events, garden parties, dinners, and investitures every year. It is not only a residence, but the central hub of a working monarchy.

The balcony is extra special as it is the most "public" part of the palace. It has been the site of numerous celebrations of some of the most important occasions in British history, including the end of World War II, when King George VI, Queen Elizabeth, Princess Elizabeth, and Princess Margaret, joined by Prime Minister Winston Churchill, appeared on the balcony to a cheering crowd of thousands to celebrate Germany's surrender in May 1945. Numerous royal couples have also appeared on the balcony on their wedding day to greet well-wishers, smiling and using their best royal waves! Buckingham Palace is open to the public during August and September each year while the Queen is on her annual summer holiday at Balmoral Castle in Scotland.

Windsor Castle—Official Royal Residence

The oldest official royal residence still in use today is Windsor Castle. It is located in the picturesque town of Windsor, about twenty miles outside of London. With its imposing gray stone walls and large circular tower, it evokes thoughts of King Arthur and his Knights of the Round Table. Its construction began almost one thousand years ago under William the Conqueror in 1070. Unsurprisingly, it took about sixteen years to finish. It has been a home to thirty-nine British monarchs over a span of 900 years! Like Buckingham Palace, it continues to be not only a home, but also a working residence for official duties performed by the Queen and other members of the royal family. The Queen often spends her weekends at Windsor Castle, and it is said to be her favorite royal residence, holding many happy memories from her childhood.

Windsor Castle has a vast and varied history. It was one of the favorite residences of Queen Victoria and Prince Albert, and they spent much of their time there. Unfortunately, it also has some tragic associations, being the location of Prince Albert's death from typhoid at age forty-two in 1861, leading to Queen Victoria's lifelong state of mourning. During World War II, the then Princess Elizabeth and her sister Princess Margaret moved to Windsor Castle for their safety. Their parents remained at Buckingham Palace in London during the week, but traveled to Windsor in the evenings and on weekends to be with their daughters.

On November 20, 1992—the Queen and the Duke of Edinburgh's forty-fifth wedding anniversary—a massive fire broke out at the castle and spread extremely quickly, obliterating 115 rooms, including nine state rooms. It took fifteen hours to finally put out the blaze. The Queen was utterly devastated by the destruction. Thankfully, many pieces of priceless artwork had been rescued from the fire. Restoration work began almost immediately under the supervision of the Duke of Edinburgh and was completed exactly five years later on the Queen and Duke of Edinburgh's fiftieth wedding anniversary.

Windsor Castle is very famous for the large St. George's Chapel. Ten monarchs are buried there, including King Henry VIII, King Edward VII, King George V (the Queen's grandfather), and King George VI (the Queen's father). Queen Mary (the Queen's grandmother and wife of King George V) and Queen Elizabeth, the Queen Mother, are also buried there, as is the Queen's sister Princess Margaret.

The chapel has also been the site of numerous royal weddings, including the wedding of the Queen's youngest son Prince Edward to Sophie Rhys-Jones in 1999. The Queen's eldest grandchild Peter Phillips married Autumn Kelly at St. George's Chapel in 2008. More recently, it was the site of the fairytale wedding of Prince Harry to

American actress Meghan Markle in May 2018 and the wedding of Princess Eugenie to Jack Brooksbank in October 2018. These recent royal weddings have significantly increased Windsor Castle's popularity as a tourist attraction. While many royal couples have been married at Westminster Abbey in London, St. George's Chapel is smaller and tends to offer a more private, intimate feel.

Kensington Palace—Official Royal Residence

Known today most famously as the home of the Duke and Duchess of Cambridge and their young family, Kensington Palace is a stunning brick residence surrounded by a large public park. It was purchased in 1689 by King William III, though at the time it was known as Nottingham House— another "house" that became a palace! Successive monarchs expanded it over time. It is famous as the childhood residence of Queen Victoria and was also where she learned of her accession to the throne at the age of eighteen on June 20, 1837. The last monarch, however, to use the palace as a residence was King George II over 250 years ago. Since then it has served as the home to numerous extended members of the royal family. Princess Margaret and her husband Antony Armstrong-Jones made their home at Kensington Palace, and Margaret continued to live there after their divorce. Prince Charles and Princess Diana also called Kensington Palace home after their 1981 marriage. Prince William and Prince Harry grew up at the palace, and it remained the home of their mother, the Princess of Wales, until her tragic death in 1997.

Kensington Palace can easily be described as a "royal dormitory," housing multiple members of the royal family with individual residences varying greatly in size. The Duke and Duchess of Cambridge live in a sprawling twenty-room "apartment" known as Apartment 1A with their three young children, whereas the Duke and Duchess of Sussex, who lived at the palace during their engagement and for about a year after their marriage, occupied a relatively small two-bedroom home known as Nottingham Cottage. Other members of the royal family who live at Kensington Palace are Princess Eugenie and Jack Brooksbank residing in Ivy Cottage, the Duke and Duchess of Gloucester, the Duke and Duchess of Kent, and Prince and Princess Michael of Kent.

The Palace of Holyroodhouse—Official Royal Residence

One of the lesser known royal residences, the Palace of Holyroodhouse is located in Edinburgh and is the Queen's official royal residence in Scotland. The site dates back to about 1128 when an abbey was built there by David I. It wasn't until the reign of James IV in the early sixteenth century that the abbey and surrounding buildings and structures were converted into a palace. It is a stunning residence and was greatly modernized during the reign of King George V in the early twentieth century. It is open to the public all year, except when the Queen is in residence—which is not very often. She attends Holyrood Week at the end of June and beginning of July to carry out various engagements celebrating Scottish culture and history. But other than that, her time spent at Holyroodhouse is rather limited. The Queen's eldest granddaughter Zara Tindall held her wedding reception at the palace in 2011 after marrying fiancé Mike Tindall at Canongate Kirk, a church just up the street from the palace.

Balmoral Castle—Private Residence

Balmoral Castle is the Scottish holiday home of the British royal family. The estate was purchased by Prince Albert for Queen Victoria in 1852 after the pair had fallen in love with the beauty of Scotland in 1842. The home originally on the property was not seen as large enough to accommodate the royal household, so a new home needed to be built. Construction on Balmoral Castle began in 1853 and was finished in 1856. Queen Victoria adored the castle and referred to it in her diary as her "dear paradise in the Highlands." It is perhaps the most fairytale-like of all the royal residences, made of gray stone with majestic turrets and surrounded by the stunning Scottish countryside.

The Queen spends her summer holiday during August and September at Balmoral. It is a massive estate (almost 50,000 acres!) and a peaceful, private retreat for Her Majesty, who enjoys being joined by many members of her family while there. Riding, shooting, fishing, and picnics are just a few of the many activities the family enjoys while vacationing on the large estate, and Prince Philip apparently loves to show off his skills on the grill! Prince Charles and Princess Diana spent a portion of their honeymoon at Balmoral. It is also remembered, unfortunately, as the place where Prince William and Prince Harry were staying in August 1997 when they were told of their mother's untimely death in a tragic car accident.

Sandringham House—Private Residence

The Sandringham Estate is the royal family's private country retreat in Norfolk and spans about 20,000 acres—a modest size compared to Balmoral! The property was originally bought for Albert Edward, Prince of Wales (later King Edward VII), by his mother Queen Victoria. The Prince of Wales and his new bride Princess Alexandra of Denmark moved into the home on the estate in 1863 a few weeks after their wedding. However, the home was quickly dubbed inadequate for their needs and torn down, with the new and current house being completed in 1870.

The estate has been passed down to successive monarchs throughout the past 150 years and has been a most beloved home to the royal family. King Edward VII's son, King George V, described Sandringham as, "the place I love better than anywhere else in the world." The Queen's father King George VI also spoke sentimentally of

Sandringham, saying, "I have always been happy here and I love the place."

While it has been a home filled with joy for members of the royal family, it has also been the site of tragedy. The Queen's grandfather King George V died there in 1936, and her father King George VI passed away in his sleep at Sandringham in 1952.

Sandringham is most well-known today as the home where the royal family spends Christmas. (The Queen's first televised Christmas message was delivered from Sandringham in 1957.) The Queen arrives at the estate shortly before Christmas and stays through February 6, the anniversary of her father's death as well as the anniversary of the day she became queen. The family attends Christmas day services at the Church of St. Mary Magdalene on the estate, walking from the main house along a path to the church where lines of well-wishers come to see and greet the royal family members. It is also a chance to catch a glimpse of new members of the royal family, including the Duchess of Cambridge in 2011, following her marriage to Prince William that April. In a somewhat surprising break with precedent, Meghan Markle walked to the church in 2017 with Prince Harry, while the couple was engaged but not yet married.

The small, cozy church was also where the christening of Her Royal Highness Princess Charlotte of Cambridge took place in July 2015. Sweet little Charlotte was pushed in a shining black baby carriage by her mother the Duchess of Cambridge with her father Prince William and older brother Prince George—feisty and adorable—following along beside.

Sandringham House itself is only one of many residences on the estate. The Duke and Duchess of Cambridge were given Anmer Hall, a large house on the estate, by the Queen as a wedding gift following their nuptials in April 2011. The Georgian-style home was built in 1802 and has ten bedrooms along with tennis courts and a swimming pool. While Kensington Palace in London is the official residence of the Duke and Duchess of Cambridge and their young family, Anmer Hall is a peaceful country retreat that offers them a greater degree of privacy.

Bonus—The Royal Yacht *Britannia*:
The Queen's "Floating Palace"

HMY *Britannia* was launched officially on April 16, 1953, in Scotland. It was used by the royal family for over forty years and traveled over one million nautical miles. It was used not only for family holidays, but also for official events, such as state visits and receptions. It took around 250 crewmembers to keep *Britannia* running in ship-shape condition. Four royal honeymoons took place on *Britannia*, including that of Princess Margaret and Antony Armstrong-Jones in 1960 as well as the honeymoon of the Prince and Princess of Wales in 1981.

Members of the royal family traveled on *Britannia* for an astonishing 968 state visits. The Queen has entertained numerous iconic historical figures aboard the yacht, including Ronald Reagan, Winston Churchill, and Nelson Mandela. But *Britannia* was also a traveling home for the royal family and held many special memories. The Queen and Duke of Edinburgh had a large hand in the design of the various rooms and spent countless hours aboard with their children and grandchildren. They enjoyed picnics on remote islands, an inflatable pool on the large Verandah

Deck, water fights, and numerous other games. It allowed the family an enormous level of privacy, and the Queen has said that *Britannia* was "the one place I can truly relax."

The happy memories made it all the more painful when the government announced that *Britannia* was too expensive to run and would be decommissioned without a replacement. HMY *Britannia* made her final voyage in 1997 and at the decommissioning ceremony, the Queen showed an extremely rare public display of emotion when she wiped a tear from her eye.

Royal Pets

Corgis and Other Royal Canines

No royal book would be complete without a discussion of royal pets, as no one in the royal family who owns animals would consider their families complete without their furry friends. Without question, the best place to begin to learn about these four-legged friends is with the Queen's iconic corgis.

The story of the royal corgis—Pembroke Welsh corgis to be exact—begins in 1933, when a corgi puppy was

chosen from a litter by the then
Duke of York (the Queen's father)
and his young family. This corgi was
named Dookie, and the family added
a second, Jane, a few years later and
eventually Jane's puppy, Crackers. Tragically, Dookie died
at the beginning of World War II and Jane was killed when
hit by a car.

Princess Elizabeth was given her very own corgi for
her eighteenth birthday in April 1944 and named her
Susan. The pair became inseparable, with the princess even
smuggling Susan along on her honeymoon in 1947, dis-
guising her beneath some blankets in the carriage that left
Buckingham Palace for the train station. The Queen has
owned over thirty Pembroke Welsh corgis in her lifetime,
and all have descended from Susan.

Corgis have become synonymous with the Queen and
the British monarchy. For decades photos have been pub-

lished of the Queen surrounded by her short,
furry brood. Images and stuffed likenesses
of corgis can be found in countless tourist shops across London. Unfortunately,

in April 2018, the Queen's last "Susan-descended" corgi, Willow, passed away. And in October of that same year, Whisper, a corgi she adopted in 2016 upon the death of her gamekeeper Bill Fenwick, also died, bringing the reign of the royal corgis to an end.

The Queen has reportedly stopped breeding dogs, fearing that any might outlive her. She does not want them to have to go through the pain and confusion of losing an owner. However, that does not mean that there aren't any more "Queen's Best Friends" at Buckingham Palace. Her Majesty still has two dorgis, dachshund-corgi mixes, named Vulcan and Candy. The mix was created when one of Princess Margaret's dachshunds mated with one of the Queen's corgis. The Queen also has a soft spot for Labradors and cocker spaniels, owning many of them throughout her reign, which she has used as gundogs on her estates.

The Queen is not the only royal with a love of cocker spaniels. The Duke and Duchess of Cambridge became the proud owners of a black cocker spaniel puppy in late 2011, a few months after their marriage.

They dubbed the new family member Lupo, which means "wolf" in Italian. Lupo was from a litter of one of the Middletons' family dogs, and the duchess's parents gave the puppy to the couple as a gift. Lupo's importance to the growing Cambridge family has been shown often through his inclusion in numerous officially released family portraits.

While the Cambridges seem to favor cocker spaniels, the Duke and Duchess of Sussex prefer beagles and Labradors. When Meghan Markle moved to the UK to marry Prince Harry, she already owned two adopted dogs, Guy and Bogart. She left Bogart, a Labrador-shepherd mix, behind with friends when she moved across the pond, but took Guy, a beagle she had rescued from a Kentucky shelter in 2015, with her. The royal couple added to the family with the adoption of a Labrador puppy a few months after their marriage in 2018. The breed is beloved by Prince Harry, who, with his brother Prince William, grew up with a pet Labrador.

QUEEN ELIZABETH II — **PHILIP, DUKE OF EDINBURGH**

CHARLES, PRINCE OF WALES
- Diana, Princess of Wales
- Camilla, Duchess of Cornwall

WILLIAM, DUKE OF CAMBRIDGE
- Catherine, Duchess of Cambridge
- Prince George of Cambridge
- Princess Charlotte of Cambridge
- Prince Louis of Cambridge

HARRY, DUKE OF SUSSEX
- Meghan, Duchess of Sussex
- Archie Harrison

ANNE PRINCESS ROYAL
- Captain Mark Phillips
- Vice-Admiral Timothy Laurence

PETER PHILLIPS
- Autumn Phillips
- Savannah
- Isla

ZARA TINDALL
- Mike Tindall
- Mia Grace
- Lena Elizabeth

ANDREW, DUKE OF YORK
- Sarah, Duchess of York

PRINCESS BEATRICE OF YORK

PRINCESS EUGENIE OF YORK
- Jack Brooksbank

EDWARD EARL OF WESSEX
- Sophie, Countess of Wessex

LADY LOUISE WINDSOR

JAMES, VISCOUNT SEVERN

Royal Family
Quick Stats!

Queen Elizabeth II

FULL NAME: Elizabeth Alexandra Mary

BORN: April 21, 1926

SPOUSE: Prince Philip, Duke of Edinburgh (m. 1947–present)

CHILDREN: Prince Charles (b. 1948), Princess Anne (b. 1950), Prince Andrew (b. 1960), Prince Edward (b. 1964)

EDUCATION: Educated at home by governesses, also received lessons from Henry Martin at Eton College in constitutional history and law, studied religion under the Archbishop of Canterbury.

PASSIONS/INTERESTS: Horse racing, equestrianism, dogs, hunting, dancing, supporting the British Commonwealth through numerous charities and patronages

A RIGHT ROYAL FACT: The Queen served as an auto mechanic during World War II, and she is still the only female royal family member to have ever served in the armed forces. She also has the distinction of being the only living head of state worldwide to have served in World War II.

Prince Philip
(The Duke of Edinburgh)

FULL NAME: Philip Mountbatten

BORN: June 10, 1921

SPOUSE: Queen Elizabeth II (m. 1947)

CHILDREN: Prince Charles (b. 1948), Princess Anne
(b. 1950), Prince Andrew (b. 1960), Prince Edward
(b. 1964)

EDUCATION: MacJannet American School, Cheam
School, Gordonstoun School, and the Royal Naval
College Dartmouth

PASSIONS/INTERESTS: Sailing, carriage driving,
science, engineering, polo, piloting, conservation and
environmentalism, aiding young people

A RIGHT ROYAL FACT: Originally known as Prince
Philip of Greece and Denmark, he renounced his titles
and became a British citizen in order to marry Princess
Elizabeth (Queen Elizabeth II) in 1947.

Prince Charles
(The Prince of Wales)

FULL NAME: Charles Philip Arthur George

BORN: November 14, 1948

RELATIONSHIP TO THE QUEEN: Eldest child

SPOUSE(S): Lady Diana Spencer (m. 1981–1996, divorced), Camilla Parker Bowles (m. 2005–present)

CHILDREN: Prince William (b. 1982) and Prince Harry (b. 1984)

EDUCATION: Hill House, Cheam School, Gordonstoun School, Cambridge University, and the Royal Naval College Dartmouth

PASSIONS/INTERESTS: Helping young people and the disadvantaged, environmental protection and sustainability, watercolor painting, gardening, and the arts

A RIGHT ROYAL FACT: Prince Charles became heir apparent at age three and is the longest-serving Prince of Wales of British history.

Diana, Princess of Wales

FULL NAME: Diana Frances Spencer

BORN: July 1, 1961

DEATH: August 31, 1997

RELATIONSHIP TO THE QUEEN: Daughter-in-law

SPOUSE: Prince Charles (m. 1981–1996, divorced)

CHILDREN: Prince William (b. 1982) and Prince Harry (b. 1984)

EDUCATION: Riddlesworth Hall, West Heath School, and Chateau d'Oex (Switzerland)

PASSIONS/INTERESTS: Dancing, disadvantaged children, the homeless, AIDS victims, and the removal of land mines from war-torn areas

A RIGHT ROYAL FACT: Diana's parents rented a house on the Sandringham Estate, and she grew up with Prince Andrew and Prince Edward as playmates.

Camilla, Duchess of Cornwall

FULL NAME: Camilla Rosemary Shand (Camilla Parker Bowles after her first marriage)

BORN: July 17, 1947

RELATIONSHIP TO THE QUEEN: Daughter-in-law

SPOUSE: Andrew Parker Bowles (m. 1973–1995, divorced), Prince Charles (m. 2005–present)

CHILDREN: Thomas Henry Parker Bowles (b. 1974) and Laura Parker Bowles (b. 1978)

EDUCATION: Dumbrells School, Queen's Gate School, Mon Fertile School (Switzerland), and Institut Britannique (France)

PASSIONS/INTERESTS: Fishing, cross-country skiing, gardening, animal rescue, aiding victims of sexual abuse and domestic violence, literacy, and female empowerment

A RIGHT ROYAL FACT: The Duchess of Cornwall owns two rescue dogs, both Jack Russell terriers, named Beth and Bluebell.

Prince William
(The Duke of Cambridge)

FULL NAME: William Arthur Philip Louis

BORN: June 21, 1982

RELATIONSHIP TO THE QUEEN: Third grandchild, second grandson

SPOUSE: Catherine Elizabeth Middleton (m. 2011)

CHILDREN: Prince George (b. 2013), Princess Charlotte (b. 2015), Prince Louis (b. 2018)

EDUCATION: Mrs. Mynors Nursery School, Wetherby Preparatory School, Ludgrove School, Eton College, St. Andrews University, and the Royal Military Academy Sandhurst

PASSIONS/INTERESTS: Football, tennis, polo, mental health awareness, conservation, help for young people, and supporting the armed forces

A RIGHT ROYAL FACT: Prince William served as an RAF search and rescue pilot for three years and then two years as an air ambulance pilot.

Catherine, Duchess of Cambridge

FULL NAME: Catherine Elizabeth Middleton

BORN: January 9, 1982

RELATIONSHIP TO THE QUEEN: Granddaughter-in-law

SPOUSE: Prince William (m. 2011)

CHILDREN: Prince George (b. 2013), Princess Charlotte (b. 2015), Prince Louis (b. 2018)

EDUCATION: St. Andrew's School, Marlborough College, and the University of St. Andrews

PASSIONS/INTERESTS: Art, photography, tennis, hockey, nature, families, mental health awareness, and child hospital and hospice care

A RIGHT ROYAL FACT: As a child, the Duchess of Cambridge spent a period of time living in Amman, Jordan, while her father was based there working for British Airways.

Prince George of Cambridge

FULL NAME: George Alexander Louis

BORN: July 22, 2013

RELATIONSHIP TO THE QUEEN: Third great-grandchild, first great-grandson

EDUCATION: Westacre Montessori School, Thomas's Battersea School

A RIGHT ROYAL FACT: Prince George's first "royal tour" was to Australia and New Zealand with his parents in 2014.

Princess Charlotte of Cambridge

FULL NAME: Charlotte Elizabeth Diana

BORN: May 2, 2015

RELATIONSHIP TO THE QUEEN: Fifth great-grandchild, fourth great-granddaughter

EDUCATION: Willcocks Nursery School, Thomas's Battersea School

A RIGHT ROYAL FACT: Princess Charlotte's first "holiday" with her family was on a skiing trip to the French Alps in 2016.

Prince Louis of Cambridge

FULL NAME: Louis Arthur Charles

BORN: April 23, 2018

RELATIONSHIP TO THE QUEEN: Sixth great-grandchild, second great-grandson

A RIGHT ROYAL FACT: Prince Louis delighted royal watchers with his array of adorable faces during his first appearance on the Buckingham Palace balcony in June 2019 for Trooping the Colour.

Prince Harry
(The Duke of Sussex)

FULL NAME: Henry Charles Albert David

BORN: September 15, 1984

RELATIONSHIP TO THE QUEEN: Fourth grandchild, third grandson

SPOUSE: Meghan Markle (m. 2018)

CHILDREN: Archie Harrison Mountbatten-Windsor (b. 2019)

EDUCATION: Mrs. Mynors Nursery School, Wetherby Preparatory School, Ludgrove School, Eton College, and the Royal Military Academy Sandhurst

PASSIONS/INTERESTS: Rugby, football, polo, conservation, children, various causes in Africa, support for servicemen and women, environmental protection, and mental health awareness

A RIGHT ROYAL FACT: Prince Harry served for ten years in the British Armed Forces, including two active tours in Afghanistan.

Meghan, Duchess of Sussex

FULL NAME: Rachel Meghan Markle

BORN: August 4, 1981

RELATIONSHIP TO THE QUEEN: Granddaughter-in-law

SPOUSE: Prince Harry (m. 2018)

CHILDREN: Archie Harrison Mountbatten-Windsor (b. 2019)

EDUCATION: Hollywood Little Red Schoolhouse, Immaculate Heart High School, Northwestern University

PASSIONS/INTERESTS: Acting, fashion design, environmental protection, gender equality, women's empowerment, and social justice

A RIGHT ROYAL FACT: The Duchess of Sussex learned to speak Spanish while interning at the US Embassy in Argentina. She also studied French for six years.

Archie Montbatten-Windsor

FULL NAME: Archie Harrison Mountbatten-Windsor

BORN: May 6, 2019

RELATIONSHIP TO THE QUEEN: Eighth great-grandchild, third great-grandson

A RIGHT ROYAL FACT: Archie's first "royal tour" was to South Africa with his parents in September 2019.

Princess Anne
(The Princess Royal)

FULL NAME: Anne Elizabeth Alice Louise

BORN: August 15, 1950

RELATIONSHIP TO THE QUEEN: Second child, only daughter

SPOUSE(S): Captain Mark Phillips (m. 1973–1992, divorced), Admiral Timothy Laurence (m. 1992–present)

CHILDREN: Peter Phillips (b. 1977) and Zara Phillips (b. 1981)

EDUCATION: Princess Anne was educated privately at Buckingham Palace as a child and then attended and graduated from Benenden School.

PASSIONS/INTERESTS: Horse racing and equestrianism, children, providing support for caregivers, and aid for better transportation in developing nations

A RIGHT ROYAL FACT: Princess Anne qualified for the British equestrian team and competed at the 1976 Olympics in Montreal.

Peter Phillips

FULL NAME: Peter Mark Andrew Phillips

BORN: November 15, 1977

RELATIONSHIP TO THE QUEEN: First grandchild

SPOUSE: Autumn Kelly (m. 2008–2020, divorce pending)

CHILDREN: Savannah Phillips (b. 2010) and Isla Phillips (b. 2012)

EDUCATION: University of Exeter

A RIGHT ROYAL FACT: He and his sister Zara are the only two of the Queen's eight grandchildren who do not have titles.

Zara Phillips (Tindall)

FULL NAME: Zara Anne Elizabeth Tindall

BORN: May 15, 1981

RELATIONSHIP TO THE QUEEN: Second grandchild, first granddaughter

SPOUSE: Mike Tindall (m. 2011)

CHILDREN: Mia Tindall (b. 2014) and Lena Tindall (b. 2018)

EDUCATION: University of Exeter

A RIGHT ROYAL FACT: Zara won a silver medal in the London Olympics in 2012 as part of the British equestrian team.

Prince Andrew (The Duke of York)

FULL NAME: Andrew Albert Christian Edward

BORN: February 19, 1960

RELATIONSHIP TO THE QUEEN: Third child, second son

SPOUSE: Sarah Ferguson (m. 1986–1996, divorced)

CHILDREN: Princess Beatrice (b. 1988) and Princess Eugenie (b. 1990)

EDUCATION: Heatherdown Preparatory School, Gordonstoun School, and the Royal Naval College Dartmouth

PASSIONS/INTERESTS: Golf, entrepreneurship, trade and investment, and support for members of the armed services

A RIGHT ROYAL FACT: The Duke of York served as a helicopter pilot in 1982 during the Falklands War.

Princess Beatrice of York

FULL NAME: Beatrice Elizabeth Mary

BORN: August 8, 1988

RELATIONSHIP TO THE QUEEN: Fifth grandchild, second granddaughter

SPOUSE: Edoardo Mapelli Mozzi (betrothed 2019)

EDUCATION: Upton House School, Coworth Park School, St. George's School, and Goldsmiths, University of London

PASSIONS/INTERESTS: History, aid for children in poverty, childhood literacy

A RIGHT ROYAL FACT: Princess Beatrice played an extra in the film *The Young Victoria* (2009) about her great-great-great-great grandmother, Queen Victoria.

Princess Eugenie of York

FULL NAME: Eugenie Victoria Helena

BORN: March 23, 1990

RELATIONSHIP TO THE QUEEN: Sixth grandchild, third granddaughter

SPOUSE: Jack Brooksbank (m. 2018)

EDUCATION: Upton House School, Coworth Park School, St. George's School, Marlborough College, and Newcastle University

PASSIONS/INTERESTS: English literature, art history, orthopedic research, eliminating plastic pollution, and combating modern slavery

A RIGHT ROYAL FACT: Princess Eugenie had to have surgery as a child to correct a curvature in her spine resulting from scoliosis. She has two titanium rods in her back as a result.

Prince Edward
(The Earl of Wessex)

FULL NAME: Edward Antony Richard Louis

BORN: March 10, 1964

RELATIONSHIP TO THE QUEEN: Fourth child, third son

SPOUSE: Sophie Rhys-Jones (m. 1999–present)

CHILDREN: Lady Louise (b. 2003) and James, Viscount Severn (b. 2007)

EDUCATION: Gibbs School, Heatherdown Preparatory School, Gordonstoun School, and Cambridge University

PASSIONS/INTERESTS: History, gardening, television production, tennis and other sports, support for young people, and the arts

A RIGHT ROYAL FACT: Prince Edward once owned his own television production company known as Ardent Productions before taking on full-time royal duties in 2002.

Sophie, Countess of Wessex

FULL NAME: Sophie Helen Rhys-Jones

BORN: January 20, 1965

RELATIONSHIP TO THE QUEEN: Daughter-in-law

SPOUSE: Prince Edward (m. 1999)

CHILDREN: Lady Louise (b. 2003) and James, Viscount Severn (b. 2007)

EDUCATION: Dulwich College Preparatory School, Kent College School for Girls, and West Kent College

PASSIONS/INTERESTS: Fashion, tennis, agriculture, support for children with disabilities, eliminating avoidable blindness, and aid to victims of sexual violence

A RIGHT ROYAL FACT: Sophie has a very strong bond with the Queen and is said to be one of her closest confidants.

Lady Louise Windsor

FULL NAME: Louise Alice Elizabeth Mary Mountbatten-Windsor

BORN: November 8, 2003

RELATIONSHIP TO THE QUEEN: Seventh grandchild, fourth granddaughter

A RIGHT ROYAL FACT: Lady Louise served as one of four bridesmaids in the wedding of Prince William and Catherine Middleton in 2011.

James, Viscount Severn

FULL NAME: James Alexander Philip Theo Mountbatten-Windsor

BORN: December 17, 2007

RELATIONSHIP TO THE QUEEN: Eighth grandchild, fourth grandson

A RIGHT ROYAL FACT: In 2018, James served as a special attendant along with his sister in two of his cousins' weddings—Prince Harry and Princess Eugenie.

Notes

"About Balmoral: The History of the Scottish Holiday Home to the Royal Family." *Balmoral: Scottish Home to the Royal Family*, Balmoral Estates, 2019, www.balmoralcastle.com/about.htm.

Abraham, Tamara. "The Most Epic Royal Jewelry in History." *Harper's Bazaar*, 10 Oct. 2018, www.harpersbazaar.com/wedding/bridal-fashion/g23656976/best-royal-family-jewelry-of-all-time/?slide=3.

Acott Williams, Claudia. "Queen Victoria and Jewelry." *Sotheby's*, 27 July 2018, www.sothebys.com/en/articles/queen-victoria-and-jewelry.

Adebowale, Temi. "All the Residences Owned by the British Royal Family." *Harper's Bazaar*, 11 Sept. 2018, www.harpersbazaar.com/celebrity/latest/g22573559/royal-family-residences-homes-properties/.

Aquino, Gabriel. "Why are Prince Edward's Children Not Titled as Prince and Princess?" *Royal Central*, 31 May 2018, royalcentral.co.uk/uk/why-prince-edwards-children-are-not-titled-prince-and-princess-103666/.

Arnold, Adam. "Queen Says Riding in Her Gold State Coach is 'Horrible' Experience." *Sky News*, Sky UK, 12 Jan. 2018, news.sky.com/story/queen-says-riding-in-her-gold-state-coach-is-horrible-experience-11203973.

Aronson, Theo. *Grandmama of Europe: The Crowned Descendants of Queen Victoria*. London, Thistle Publishing, 2014.

Baker, Keiligh. "Royal Baby: What Do We Know about Archie's Christening?" *BBC News*, 6 July 2019, www.bbc.com/news/uk-48881697.

Begley, Sarah. "The White Dress That Changed Wedding History Forever." *Time*, 10 Feb. 2015, time.com/3698249/white-weddings/.

Bhardwa, Seeta. "Where Did UK Royals Go to University?" *The World University Rankings*, Times Higher Education, 1 Dec. 2017, www.timeshighereducation.com/student/blogs/where-did-uk-royals-go-university#survey-answer.

Bonner, Mehera. "17 Beautiful Tiaras Owned by the Royal Family." *Harper's Bazaar Australia*, 20 Aug. 2017, www.harpersbazaar.com.au/culture/17-tiaras-owned-by-royals-14101.

Bruner, Raisa. "Analyzing Every Tiara Meghan Markle Could Wear at the Royal Wedding." *Time*, 3 May 2018, time.com/5237031/meghan-markle-tiara/.

Bryant, Kenzie. "All the Queen's Corgis Are Gone, so God Save the Dorgis." *Vanity Fair*, 26 Oct. 2018, www.vanityfair.com/style/2018/10/queens-corgis-whisper-died-long-live-dorgis.

Bryant, Kenzie, et al. "21 Times Queen Elizabeth Wore Exactly the Right Thing to a Wedding." *Vanity Fair*, 4 May 2018, www.vanityfair.com/style/photos/2018/05/queen-elizabeth-ii-wedding-guest-mother-of-the-bride-groom.

"Buckingham Palace Canadian Maple-Leaf Brooch." *The Royal Collection Shop*, Royal Collection Enterprises Limited, 2019, www.royalcollection shop.co.uk/buckingham-palace-canadian-maple-leaf-brooch.html.

Bullen, Annie. *Her Majesty Queen Elizabeth II*. Great Britain, Pitkin Publishing, 2012.

Cahn, Lauren. "This Is the Difference Between a Prince and a Duke." *Reader's Digest*, 2019, www.rd.com/culture/difference-between-a-prince-and-a-duke/.

"Cecil Beaton: Royal Photographer." *The V&A*, The Victoria and Albert Museum, www.vam.ac.uk/articles/cecil-beaton-royal-photographer.

Chan, Emily. "What Will Archie Harrison's Christening Look Like?" *Vogue*, 5 July 2015, www.vogue.co.uk/article/what-will-the-royal-babys-christening-look-like.

Chang, Mahalia. "12 Significant Pieces of Jewelry Duchess Catherine has Borrowed from the Royal Vault." *Harper's Bazaar Australia*, 23 Oct. 2018, www.harpersbazaar.com.au/celebrity/kate-middleton-royal-jewels-13761.

Churchill, Winston. "For Valour: King George VI." The International Churchill Society, 7 Feb. 1952, London, winstonchurchill.org/publications/finest-hour/finest-hour-114/for-valour-king-george-vi-in-remembrance-of-his-late-majesty/.

Clark, Lucie. "Queen Elizabeth II's Tiara Broke Before Her Wedding and She Dealt with it Like the Queen She Is." *Vogue Australia*, 3 May 2018, www.vogue.com.au/brides/news/queen-elizabeth-iis-tiara-broke-before-her-wedding-and-she-dealt-with-it-like-the-queen-she-is/news-story/2d7eccf873d79205ae6ff54d585a2a52.

"A Close Look at the British Royal Family's Engagement Rings." *Vogue*, 26 Sept. 2019, www.vogue.com/slideshow/british-royal-family-engagement-rings.

Cohen, Jennie. "8 Things You May Not Know About Queen Elizabeth II." *History*, A&E Television Networks, 3 June 2019, www.history.com/news/8-things-you-may-not-know-about-queen-elizabeth-ii.

"Coronation." *The Official Website of the British Royal Family*, The Royal Household of Buckingham Palace, 2019, www.royal.uk/coronation.

"Coronations." *Westminster Abbey*, Dean and Chapter of Westminster, 2019, www.westminster-abbey.org/about-the-abbey/history/royalty/coronations.

Correia, Roberta. "Prince Charles and Princess Diana's Wedding in Photos." *Brides*, Dotdash Publishing, 15 Mar. 2018, www.brides.com/gallery/princess-diana-prince-charles-royal-wedding.

"The Countess of Wessex." *The Official Website of the British Royal Family*, The Royal Household of Buckingham Palace, 2019, www.royal.uk/the-countess-of-wessex.

"Crown Office." *The Gazette: Official Public Record*, TSO, a Williams Lea Company, 31 Dec. 2012, www.thegazette.co.uk/notice/L-60384-1738680.

Dangremond, Sam. "Looking Back at Royal Births Throughout History." *Town & Country*, 6 May 2019, www.townandcountrymag.com/society/tradition/g19724335/royal-births-history/.

Deerwester, Jayme. "Timeline: Princess Diana's Life and the Events that Made Her Who She Was." *US Today*, Gannett, 23 Aug. 2017, www.usatoday.com/story/life/people/2017/08/23/timeline-princess-dianas-life/508263001/.

Delderfield, Eric R. *Kings and Queens of England and Great Britain*. David & Charles Publishers, 1977, p. 126.

"Delhi Durbar Tiara." *The Royal Collection Trust*, 2019, www.rct.uk/collection/themes/exhibitions/diamonds-a-jubilee-celebration/buckingham-palace/delhi-durbar-tiara.

"Diana, Princess of Wales." Encyclopedia Britannica, 2019, https://www.britannica.com/biography/Diana-princess-of-Wales.

"The Duchess of Cambridge." *The Official Website of the British Royal Family*, The Royal Household of Buckingham Palace, 2019, www.royal.uk/the-duchess-of-cambridge.

"The Duchess of Sussex." *The Official Website of the British Royal Family*, The Royal Household of Buckingham Palace, 2019, www.royal.uk/the-duchess-of-sussex.

"The Duke of Cambridge." *The Official Website of the British Royal Family*, The Royal Household, 2019, www.royal.uk/the-duke-of-cambridge.

"The Duke of Edinburgh." *The Official Website of the British Royal Family*, The Royal Household of Buckingham Palace, 2019, www.royal.uk/the-duke-of-edinburgh.

"The Duke of Sussex." *The Official Website of the British Royal Family*, The

Royal Household of Buckingham Palace, 2019, www.royal.uk/the-duke-of-sussex.

"The Duke of York." *The Official Website of the British Royal Family*, The Royal Household of Buckingham Palace, 2019, www.royal.uk/the-duke-york.

Durand, Carolyn, and Katie Kindelan. "Puppy in the Palace: Prince Harry, Duchess Meghan Get a New Dog." *ABC News*, 27 Aug. 2018, abcnews.go.com/GMA/Culture/puppy-palace-prince-harry-duchess-meghan-dog/story?id=57422105.

"Earl of Wessex." *Debrett's*, Debrett's LTD, 2019, www.debretts.com/the-royal-family/earl-of-wessex/.

"The Earl of Wessex." *The Official Website of the British Royal Family*, The Royal Household of Buckingham Palace, 2019, www.royal.uk/the-earl-of-wessex.

"Edward VIII." *Biography*, A&E Television Networks, 10 Sept. 2019, www.biography.com/royalty/edward-viii.

Edwards, Anne. *Matriarch: Queen Mary and the House of Windsor*. London, Rowman & Littlefield, 2015.

Field, Leslie. *The Jewels of Queen Elizabeth II: Her Personal Collection*. Harry N. Abrams, Inc., 1992.

"50 Facts About the Queen's Coronation." *The Official Website of the British Royal Family*, The Royal Household of Buckingham Palace, 2019, www.royal.uk/50-facts-about-queens-coronation-0.

"The Fire at Windsor Castle." *The Royal Collection Trust*, 2019, www.rct.uk/visit/windsor-castle/who-built-windsor-castle#/.

"A Floating Palace." *The Royal Yacht Britannia*, 2019, www.royalyacht britannia.co.uk/about/.

Foussianes, Chloe. "Queen Elizabeth's Last Corgi Has Died." *Town & Country*, 26 Oct. 2018, www.townandcountrymag.com/society/tradition/a24266696/queen-elizabeth-last-corgi-whisper-died/.

Foussianes, Chloe, and Jennifer Newman. "How Queen Elizabeth, Kate Middleton, and More Royals Have Worn the Family's Heirloom Jewelry." *Town & Country*, 20 Jan. 2019, www.townandcountrymag.com/style/jewelry-and-watches/g25939782/royal-family-jewelry/.

Frost, Katie. "Looking Back at Princess Margaret's Wedding Day." *Town & Country*, 10 Dec. 2017, www.townandcountrymag.com/society/tradition/a12265404/princess-margaret-wedding-to-lord-snowdon/.

Frost, Katie. "The True Story of Princess Margaret and Antony Armstrong-

Jones's Love Affair." *Town & Country*, 8 Dec. 2017, www. townandcountrymag.com/society/news/a9255/princess-margaret-lord-snowdon-relationship/.

Gay, Danielle. "Inside The Queen Mother and King George VI's 1923 Wedding." *Vogue*, 26 Apr. 2019, www.vogue.com.au/brides/trends/inside-the-queen-mother-and-king-george-vis-1923-wedding/image-gallery/2 531ffb756279567c08b592d08247d95?pos=1.

Gold, Michael. "8 Decades of British Royal Corgis Reportedly at an End." *New York Times*, 18 Apr. 2018, www.nytimes.com/2018/04/18/world/europe/corgi-dogs-queen-elizabeth.html.

"The Gold State Coach 1762." *The Royal Collection Trust*, 2019, www.rct.uk/collection/5000048/gold-state-coach.

Gonzales, Erica. "Kate Middleton's Diamond and Pearl Necklace Is Seriously Historic." *Harper's Bazaar*, 23 Oct. 2018, www.harpersbazaar.com/celebrity/latest/a24122924/kate-middleton-diamond-pearl-necklace-queen-alexandra/.

Gonzales, Erica. "Why Prince Philip's Title Isn't King." *Harper's Bazaar*, 12 Nov. 2019, www.harpersbazaar.com/celebrity/latest/a29748471/prince-philip-title-not-king/.

Greenspan, Rachel E. "Royal Baby Archie May Not Have a Royal Title, After All. Here's Why That's Not Surprising." *Time*, 8 May 2018, time.com/5585816/royal-baby-archie-harrison-title/.

"Greeting a Member of the Royal Family." *The Official Website of the British Royal Family*, The Royal Household of Buckingham Palace, 2019, www.royal.uk/greeting-member-royal-family.

Haddon, Celia. "Her Devoted Canine Companions—Cocker Spaniels, Labradors and, of Course, Corgis." *London Telegraph*, 20 Apr. 2006, www.telegraph.co.uk/news/uknews/1400201/Her-devoted-canine-companions-cocker-spaniels-labradors-and-of-course-corgis.html.

Hallemann, Caroline. "Inside the Royals' Favorite Scottish Getaway, Balmoral Castle." *Town & Country*, 6 Aug. 2019, www.townandcountrymag.com/society/tradition/a12001419/balmoral-castle-scotland/.

Hallemann, Caroline. "The Moment Philip Became a British Prince—And Why He Isn't the King." *Town & Country*, 4 Oct. 2017, www.townandcountrymag.com/society/tradition/a12775104/why-is-prince-philip-not-king/.

"Her Children." *Queen Victoria's Empire*, Public Broadcasting Service, 2019, www.pbs.org/empires/victoria/text/majestychildren.html.

"Her Majesty the Queen." *The Official Website of the British Royal Family*, The Royal Household of Buckingham Palace, 2019, www.royal.uk/her-majesty-the-queen.

"Highlights of the Royal Mews." *The Royal Collection Trust*, 2019, www.rct.uk/visit/the-royal mews-buckingham-palace/highlights-of-the-royal-mews#/.

Hill, Duncan, et al., eds. *The Royal Family: A Year by Year Chronicle of the House of Windsor*. United Kingdom, Parragon, 2012.

Hill, Erin. "All About Princess Margaret's Lotus Flower Tiara That Is Now Worn by Princess Kate." *People*, 9 Feb. 2017, people.com/royals/all-about-princess-margarets-lotus-flower-tiara-that-is-now-worn-by-princess-kate/.

"History." *Sandringham Estate*, 2019, sandringhamestate.co.uk/history.

Hodgkin, Emily. "Is Zara Tindall a Princess? Why Doesn't She Share Eugenie and Beatrice's Title?" *Daily Express*, 18 Apr. 2019, www.express.co.uk/life-style/life/1115711/zara-tindall-princess-royal-family.

Hodgkin, Emily. "Story of Kate's 38-diamond Necklace from Foreign King with £1.5 Billion Collection." *Daily Express*, 7 June 2019, www.express.co.uk/life-style/style/1137376/kate-middleton-latest-news-pictures-royal-jewellery-queen.

"HRH The Duchess of Cornwall." *The Official Website of the British Royal Family*, Clarence House, 2019, https://www.princeofwales.gov.uk/biographies/hrh-duchess-cornwall.

"HRH The Prince of Wales." *The Official Website of the British Royal Family*, Clarence House, 2019, www.princeofwales.gov.uk/biographies/hrh-prince-wales.

Hubbard, Lauren. "The Iconic Jewels from Princess Diana's Collection That Prince Harry Could Give Meghan Markle." *Town & Country*, 28 May 2018, www.townandcountrymag.com/style/jewelry-and-watches/g20682652/princess-diana-jewelry-collection/.

Hubbard, Lauren. "Queen Victoria's Descendants Still Reign Over Europe." *Town & Country*, 17 Feb. 2019, www.townandcountrymag.com/society/tradition/a26193545/queen-victoria-descendants-on-the-throne/#.

Hufton, Catherine. "Royal Romances—The Jewelry Behind History's Greatest Love Stories." *Daily Telegraph*, 28 July 2018, www.telegraph.co.uk/luxury/jewellery/house-of-garrard/royal-romances/.

"James Windsor." *Debrett's*, Debrett's LTD, 2019, www.debretts.com/the-royal-family/james-windsor/.

Kettler, Sara. "How Prince Philip's Life Was Upended When Elizabeth Became Queen." *Biography*, A&E Television Networks, 20 Aug. 2019, www.biography.com/news/prince-philip-queen-elizabeth-marriage-relationship-sacrifices.

Kiehna, Lauren. "The Edinburgh Wedding Bracelet." *The Court Jeweller*, 11 June 2019, www.thecourtjeweller.com/2019/06/the-edinburgh-wedding-bracelet.html.

Kiehna, Lauren. "Kate's Jewelry Box: The Queen's Diamond Chandelier Earrings." *The Crown Jeweler*, 15 May 2016, www.thecourtjeweller.com/2016/05/kates-jewelry-box-queens-diamond.html.

Kriss, Randa. "The Queen's Royal Corgis." *American Kennel Club*, 7 May 2019, www.akc.org/expert-advice/lifestyle/the-queens-royal-corgis/.

"Lady Louise Windsor." *Debrett's*, Debrett's LTD, 2019, www.debretts.com/the-royal-family/lady-louise-windsor/.

Laliberte, Marissa. "How Princess Diana Forever Changed How Royal Women Give Birth." *Reader's Digest*, 2019, www.rd.com/culture/princess-diana-changed-royal-births/.

Laliberte, Marissa. "This Is the Line of Succession to the British Throne." *Reader's Digest*, 2019, www.rd.com/culture/royal-line-of-succession/page/2/.

Lee, Samantha, et al. "Prince Harry and Meghan Markle are Moving Out of Their London Palace Home: Here are the 13 Other Royals They Leave Behind." *Business Insider*, Insider Inc, 26 Nov. 2018, www.businessinsider.com/prince-harry-meghan-markle-prince-william-kate-and-11-other-royals-all-live-in-the-same-palace-2018-5.

Lowe, Lindsay. "Meghan Markle Wears Princess Diana's Butterfly Earrings and Bracelet." *Today Show*, NBC Universal, 16 Oct. 2018, www.today.com/style/former-meghan-markle-wears-princess-diana-s-butterfly-earrings-bracelet-t139837.

Luckel, Madeleine. "Queen Victoria Made White Wedding Dresses Popular. Here's What Else You Should Know About Her Royal Wedding." *Vogue*, 15 Jan. 2017, www.vogue.com/article/queen-victoria-royal-wedding-facts-victoria-premiere.

Luckel, Madeleine. "This Is the Countryside Home Where Kate Middleton and Prince William Really Live." *Vogue*, 13 Jan. 2017, www.vogue.com/article/anmer-hall-kate-middleton-prince-william.

Mackelden, Amy. "Kate Middleton Wears the Lover's Knot Tiara to State Banquet for the Trumps." *Harper's Bazaar*, 3 June 2019, www.

harpersbazaar.com/celebrity/latest/a27702612/kate-middleton-tiara-trump-state-banquet/.

Mackelden, Amy. "Meghan Markle Paid Tribute to Princess Diana at the Smart Works Collection Launch." *Harper's Bazaar*, 12 Sept. 2019, www.harpersbazaar.com/celebrity/latest/a29020384/meghan-markle-princess-diana-earrings-smart-works-launch/.

MacKenzie, Roddy. "'Monarchical No.1'—Churchill and Queen Elizabeth II." *The International Churchill Society*, winstonchurchill.org/publications/finest-hour/finest-hour-175/monarchical-no-1-churchill-and-queen-elizabeth-ii/.

Madaus, Sarah. "Sophie, the Countess of Wessex Referred to Queen Elizabeth as 'Mama' in a Speech Last Night." *Town & Country*, 30 Oct. 2019, www.townandcountrymag.com/society/tradition/a29637838/sophie-countess-of-wessex-queen-elizabeth-nickname-mama/.

Maloney, Maggie. "The 25 Most Gorgeous Royal Wedding Tiara Moments of All Time." *Town & Country*, 20 June 2019, www.townandcountrymag.com/the-scene/weddings/g17805394/royal-wedding-tiaras-throughout-history/?slide=5.

Mander-Jones, Ella. "From Queen to Countess: A Complete Guide to British Royal Titles." *Vogue*, 15 Apr. 2019, www.vogue.com.au/culture/features/all-of-the-royal-titles-explained/image-gallery/7e943b363ed9b3597df35c94b7661bcf?pos=1.

Matthews, Lauren, and Jamie Cuccinelli. "Kate Middleton and Prince William's Royal Wedding Day: A Look Back." *Brides*, Dotdash Publishing, 29 Apr. 2019, www.brides.com/gallery/royal-wedding-photos-prince-william-kate-middleton-wedding-photos.

McDonald, Jorie N. "Queen Elizabeth's Most Spectacular Jewels." *Southern Living*, 2019, www.southernliving.com/culture/celebrities/queen-elizabeth-royal-jewels.

"Meghan Markle." *Biography*, A&E Television Networks, 24 Sept. 2019, www.biography.com/royalty/meghan-markle.

Menkes, Suzy. *The Royal Jewels*. Contemporary Books, Inc., 1989.

Menza, Kaitlin, et al. "40 Royal Wedding Facts You May Have Missed from Prince William and Kate Middleton's Wedding Day." *Good Housekeeping*, 7 June 2019, www.goodhousekeeping.com/life/entertainment/g3513/royal-wedding-facts/.

Messer, Lesley, and Michael Rothman. "Full Transcript of Prince Harry and Meghan Markle's Engagement Interview." *ABC News*, 27 Nov. 2017, abcnews.go.com/Entertainment/full-transcript-prince-harry-meghan-markles-engagement-interview/story?id=51415779.

Miller, Julie. "Inside Princess Diana's Royal Wedding Fairy Tale." *Vanity Fair*, www.vanityfair.com/style/2018/04/princess-diana-royal-wedding.

Nelson, Brooke. "Why Princess Charlotte's Future Kids Won't Get Royal Titles—But Prince George's Will." *Reader's Digest*, 2019, www.rd.com/culture/princess-charlotte-kids/.

Nicholl, Katie. *Kate: The Future Queen*. 1 ed., New York, Weinstein Books, 2013.

Nix, Elizabeth. "7 Surprising Facts about Royal Births." *History*, A&E Television Networks, 8 May 2019, www.history.com/news/7-surprising-facts-about-royal-births.

Oehler, Christina. "35 Royal Wedding Bouquets Throughout History." *Brides*, Dotdash Publishing, 11 Oct. 2018, www.brides.com/gallery/royal-wedding-bouquets-throughout-history.

"The Oriental Tiara." *The Royal Collection Trust*, 2019, www.rct.uk/collection/themes/exhibitions/victoria-albert-art-love/the-queens-gallery-buckingham-palace/the-oriental-tiara.

Pearl, Diana. "Jewelry We Hope to See at the Royal Wedding—Straight From Queen Elizabeth's Collection." *People*, 7 May 2018, people.com/royals/queen-elizabeth-jewelry-collection/?slide=2371991#2371991.

Picard, Caroline. "Meghan Markle Is Wearing Queen Mary's Diamond Bandeau Tiara at the Royal Wedding." *Good Housekeeping*, 19 May 2018, www.goodhousekeeping.com/beauty/fashion/a19991637/meghan-markle-tiara-royal-wedding/.

Picard, Caroline. "The 10 Hidden Details in Kate Middleton's Wedding Dress You Totally Missed." *Good Housekeeping*, 13 Sept. 2017, www.goodhousekeeping.com/beauty/fashion/g4690/kate-middleton-wedding-dress/.

Picard, Caroline. "30 Royal Baby Traditions You Didn't Realize Existed." *Good Housekeeping*, 6 May 2019, www.goodhousekeeping.com/life/parenting/g5096/royal-family-baby-traditions/?slide=11.

Picard, Caroline. "A Timeline of Prince Harry and Meghan Markle's Relationship." *Good Housekeeping*, 8 May 2019, www.goodhousekeeping.com/life/relationships/a47735/prince-harry-and-meghan-markle-matchmaker/.

Picard, Caroline. "20 Facts About Meghan Markle's Life Before She Met Prince Harry." *Good Housekeeping*, 15 Apr. 2019, www.goodhousekeeping.

com/life/a48090/meghan-markle-facts/.

Praderio, Caroline. "Here's What It Actually Means to Be a Duchess." *Insider*,
    Insider Inc, 11 Apr. 2017, www.insider.com/what-do-royal-titles-mean-
    duke-duchess-peerage-2017-4.

"Prince Albert." *Biography*, A&E Television Networks, 21 Oct. 2019,
    www.biography.com/royalty/prince-albert.

"Prince George." *The Official Website of the British Royal Family*, The Royal
    Household of Buckingham Palace, 2019, www.royal.uk/prince-george.

"Prince Louis." *The Official Website of the British Royal Family*, The Royal
    Household of Buckingham Palace, 2019, www.royal.uk/princelouis.

"Prince Philip." *Biography*, A&E Television Networks, 27 June 2019,
    www.biography.com/royalty/prince-philip.

Prince William & Catherine Middleton. Interview by Tom Bradby.
    "Engagement Interview." UK Press Association & ABC News, 16 Nov.
    2010, abcnews.go.com/Entertainment/prince-william-kate-middleton-
    interview-transcript/story?id=12163826.

"Princess Anne." *Debrett's*, Debrett's LTD, 2019, www.debretts.com/the-
    royal-family/princess-anne/.

"Princess Beatrice." *Debrett's*, Debrett's LTD, 2019, www.debretts.com/the-
    royal-family/princess-beatrice/.

"Princess Charlotte." *The Official Website of the British Royal Family*, The
    Royal Household of Buckingham Palace, 2019, www.royal.uk/princess-
    charlotte.

"Princess Diana." *Biography*, A&E Television Networks, 28 Aug. 2019,
    www.biography.com/royalty/princess-diana.

"Princess Eugenie." *Debrett's*, Debrett's LTD, 2019, www.debretts.com/the-
    royal-family/princess-eugenie/.

"The Princess Royal." *The Official Website of the British Royal Family*, The
    Royal Household of Buckingham Palace, 2019, www.royal.uk/the-
    princess-royal.

Puente, Maria. "Why didn't Princess Eugenie's Commoner Groom Get a
    Title?" *USA Today*, Gannett, 12 Oct. 2018, www.usatoday.com/story/life/
    people/2018/10/12/how-come-princess-eugenie-commoner-groom-
    didnt-get-title/1594927002/.

"The Queen Breaks Tradition to Stay on at Sandringham." *Telegraph*,
    Telegraph Media Group Limited, 10 Feb. 2013, www.telegraph.co.uk/
    news/uknews/queen-elizabeth-II/9860633/The-Queen-breaks-
    tradition-to-stay-on-at-Sandringham.html.

"The Queen, The Church, and Other Faiths." *The Official Website of the British Royal Family*, The Royal Household of Buckingham Palace, 2019, www.royal.uk/queens-relationship-churches-england-and-scotland-and-other-faiths.

"Queen Elizabeth II: 10 Photos of the Monarch's Historical Coronation." *Biography*, A&E Television Networks, 25 June 2019, www.biography.com/news/queen-elizabeth-coronation-photos.

"Queen Mary's Bandeau Tiara." *The Royal Collection Trust*, 2019, www.rct.uk/collection/themes/exhibitions/a-royal-wedding-the-duke-and-duchess-of-sussex/palace-of-holyroodhouse/queen-marys-bandeau-tiara.

"Queen Mary's Girls of Great Britain and Ireland Tiara." *The Royal Collection Trust*, 2019, www.rct.uk/collection/themes/exhibitions/diamonds-a-jubilee-celebration/buckingham-palace/queen-marys-girls-of-great-britain-and-ireland-tiara.

Queen Victoria. "Letter from Princess Victoria to King Leopold I of the Belgians." June 1836. Queen Victoria's Diamond Jubilee Scrapbook. 2012. The Royal Archives & The Royal Collection Trust. 2019, http://www.queen-victorias-scrapbook.org/index.html.

Queen Victoria. "Queen Victoria Records Her Wedding to Prince Albert." 10 Feb. 1840. Queen Victoria's Diamond Jubilee Scrapbook. 2012. The Royal Archives & The Royal Collection Trust. 2019, http://www.queen-victorias-scrapbook.org/contents/3-5.html.

"Queen Victoria's Highland Adventures Manuscript on Show in Edinburgh." *BBC News*, 11 Mar. 2015, www.bbc.com/news/uk-scotland-edinburgh-east-fife-31826801.

Ramsdale, Suzannah. "Kate Middleton Must Curtsy to Blood Princesses by Order of the Queen." *Marie Claire*, 25 June 2012, www.marieclaire.co.uk/news/celebrity-news/kate-middleton-must-curtsy-to-blood-princesses-by-order-of-the-queen-147592.

"Ranks And Privileges Of The Peerage." *Debrett's*, Debrett's LTD, 2019, https://www.debretts.com/expertise/essential-guide-to-the-peerage/ranks-and-privileges-of-the-peerage/.

Rayner, Gordon. "Duchess of Cambridge Reveals New Puppy is Named Lupo." *The London Telegraph*, 21 Feb. 2012, www.telegraph.co.uk/news/uknews/kate-middleton/9096030/Duchess-of-Cambridge-reveals-new-puppy-is-named-Lupo.html.

Rayner, Gordon. "Queen Issues Formal Decree to Guarantee Princess Title if Duchess of Cambridge Has a Girl." *Telegraph*, 9 Jan. 2013, www.

telegraph.co.uk/news/uknews/kate-middleton/9791703/Queen-issues-formal-decree-to-guarantee-princess-title-if-Duchess-of-Cambridge-has-a-girl.html.

Reslen, Eileen. "Prince William, Kate Middleton, and Meghan Markle's Dogs Are at Windsor Ahead of the Royal Wedding." *Harper's Bazaar*, 18 May 2018, www.harpersbazaar.com/celebrity/latest/a20748158/prince-william-kate-middleton-meghan-markle-dogs-royal-wedding/.

Roberts, Kayleigh. "The Meaning Behind Princess Beatrice's Royal Title." *Harper's Bazaar*, 29 Sept. 2019, www.harpersbazaar.com/celebrity/latest/a29275685/princess-beatrice-royal-title-meaning/.

"The Royal Family." *The Royal Yacht Britannia*, 2019, www.royalyachtbritannia.co.uk/about/royal-residence/the-royal-family/.

"The Royal Family Name." *The Official Website of the British Royal Family*, The Royal Household of Buckingham Palace, 2019, www.royal.uk/royal-family-name.

"The Royal Family's Honeymoon Hotels and Destinations." *Telegraph*, Telegraph Media Group Limited, 14 Mar. 2018, www.telegraph.co.uk/travel/hotels/galleries/the-royal-familys-honeymoon-hotels-and-destinations/queen-mother-honeymoon/.

"The Royal Residence." *The Royal Yacht Britannia*, 2019, www.royalyachtbritannia.co.uk/about/.

"Royal Residences: Buckingham Palace." *The Official Website of the British Royal Family*, The Royal Household of Buckingham Palace, 2019, www.royal.uk/royal-residences-buckingham-palace.

"Royal Residences: The Palace of Holyroodhouse." *The Official Website of the British Royal Family*, The Royal Household of Buckingham Palace, 2019, https://www.royal.uk/royal-residences-palace-holyroodhouse.

"Royal Residences: Sandringham House." *The Official Website of the British Royal Family*, The Royal Household of Buckingham Palace, 2019, https://www.royal.uk/royal-residences-sandringham-house.

"Royal Residences: Windsor Castle." *The Official Website of the British Royal Family*, The Royal Household of Buckingham Palace, 2019, https://www.royal.uk/royal-residences-windsor-castle.

"Royal Wedding Whispers Deciphered by Lip Reader." *CBS News*, 29 Apr. 2011.

Samhan, Jamie. "British Nobility Titles Explained: What To Know About The U.K. Peerage System." *Huffington Post*, 20 Nov. 2017, www.huffingtonpost.ca/2017/11/20/british-nobility-titles_a_23283068/.

Samuelson, Katie, and Raisa Bruner. "Your Complete Guide to the British Royal Family Tree and Line of Succession." *Time*, 6 May 2019, time. com/5238004/royal-family-tree/.

Schultz, Colin. "Queen Victoria Dreamed Up the White Wedding Dress in 1840." *Smithsonian Magazine*, 8 Dec. 2014, www.smithsonianmag. com/smart-news/queen-victoria-sparked-white-wedding-dress-trend-1840-180953550/.

Seward, Ingrid. *My Husband and I: The Inside Story of 70 Years of the Royal Marriage*. London, Simon & Schuster, 2017.

Shawcross, William. *The Queen Mother: The Official Biography*. 1 ed., Random House, 2009.

Silverman, Hannah. "The History of Osborne Myrtle in Royal Weddings." *English Heritage*, English Heritage Charity, 26 Apr. 2018, blog.english-heritage.org.uk/osborne-myrtle-and-royal-weddings/.

Silverman, Leah. "Queen Elizabeth II's Most Glamorous Jewels and Tiaras." *Town & Country Magazine*, 19 June 2019, www.townandcountrymag. com/style/jewelry-and-watches/g14504829/queen-elizabeth-jewels-crowns-tiaras/?slide=15.

"A Sombre Farewell." *The Royal Yacht Britannia*, 2019, www. royalyachtbritannia.co.uk/about/royal-residence/decommission/.

"A Speech by the Queen on her 21st Birthday, 1947." *The Official Website of the British Royal Family*, The Royal Household of Buckingham Palace, 2019, www.royal.uk/21st-birthday-speech-21-april-1947.

"The Story of Kensington Palace." *Historic Royal Palaces*, 2019, www.hrp. org.uk/kensington-palace/history-and-stories/the-story-of-kensington-palace/#gs.5tmrq4.

Souhami, Diana. *Mrs. Keppel and Her Daughter*. St. Martin's Griffin, 2014.

Taylor, Elise. "All You Need to Know About Balmoral, the Queen's Scottish Summer Castle." *Vogue*, 22 Aug. 2019, www.vogue.com/article/balmoral-scotland-queen-elizabeth-castle-royals.

Taylor, Elise. "Prince Harry and Meghan Markle's Love Story: A Timeline." *Vogue*, 22 Mar. 2019, www.vogue.com/article/meghan-markle-prince-harry-relationship-timeline?verso=true.

Vargas, Chanel. "Everything You Need to Know About Princess Diana's Wedding." *Town & Country Magazine*, 18 May 2018, www. townandcountrymag.com/the-scene/weddings/a18205641/princess-diana-prince-charles-wedding/.

"Victoria (r. 1837–1901)." *The Official Website of the British Royal Family*," The

Royal Household of Buckingham Palace, 2019, www.royal.uk/queen-victoria.

"Visit Windsor Castle." *The Royal Collection Trust*, 2019, www.rct.uk/visit/windsor-castle/who-built-windsor-castle#/.

Waxman, Olivia B. "How a Royal Baby Is Born, From Tudor Times to Meghan Markle's Modernity." *Time*, 6 May 2019, time.com/5559841/royal-baby-birth-plan-history/.

"Wedding Carriages." *The Official Website of the British Royal Family*, The Royal Household of Buckingham Palace, 2019, www.royal.uk/wedding-carriages.

"Wedding of the Duke and Duchess of Sussex." *The Official Website of the British Royal Family*, The Royal Household of Buckingham Palace, 2019, https://www.royal.uk/royal-residences-palace-holyroodhouse.

"What is The Peerage?" *Debrett's*, Debrett's LTD, 2019, www.debretts.com/expertise/essential-guide-to-the-peerage/what-is-the-peerage/.

"Who Built Buckingham Palace?" *The Royal Collection Trust, 2019*, www.rct.uk/visit/the-state-rooms-buckingham-palace/who-built-buckingham-palace#/.

"Who Built the Palace of Holyroodhouse?" *The Royal Collection Trust*, 19 May 2019, https://www.rct.uk/visit/palace-of-holyroodhouse/who-built-the-palace-of-holyroodhouse#/.

"Who Built Windsor Castle?" *The Royal Collection Trust*, 2019, www.rct.uk/visit/windsor-castle/who-built-windsor-castle#/.

Wollan, Malia. "How to Curtsy." *New York Times Magazine*, 9 May 2018, pp. 23+, www.nytimes.com/2018/05/09/magazine/how-to-curtsy.html.

"Women Who Made History: Queen Victoria." *English Heritage*, 2019, www.english-heritage.org.uk/learn/histories/women-in-history/queen-victoria/.